THE ART OF PORTRAITS

Helen Dore

A Compilation of Works from the
BRIDGEMAN ART LIBRARY

PARRAGON

posterity. By the 18th century it was in portraiture that an artist was most likely to achieve wealth and fame.

Throughout the history of the portrait artists have experienced the same recurring preoccupations. One such was the relationship between the artist and his patron, whether an individual or an institution. When an artist was commissioned to paint a portrait he had to make sure that the client got his money's worth, to satisfy him and attract others. He had to achieve a fine balance between the way the sitter saw himself – can we ever see ourselves as others see us? – and wanted himself projected, and the artist's own perception of his subject – the two were by no means always identical!

In all portraits, too, there is the problem of the sitter's self-consciousness, which can interfere with a true likeness, and which artists have chosen to deal with in different ways. One of the most successful was to depict people in an absorbing activity, with which they can identify and become engrossed.

The problem of self-consciousness does not arise in the same way with children: indeed it is their innocence and spontaneity that make them specially rewarding subjects of portraiture. Perhaps this is why so many remarkable child portraits date from different periods.

Through history children have been painted for a variety of reasons – in early times sometimes with marriage contracts in mind, or just to join their ancestors on the walls of the family home, with or without their parents. As in all forms of portraiture, different facets of the personality could be revealed according to whether the painting was of an individual or a group: sometimes children were painted with their parents as part of the family circle, sometimes with their brothers and sisters, sometimes on their own.

The self-portrait is another special form of portraiture which tells us much about the painter's attitude to his art. Most artists who painted portraits of others have also produced likenesses of themselves, for a variety of reasons: perhaps for purely practical ones, because no other model was available or affordable, and they wanted to practise; perhaps as a gift for family or friends; to experiment with the special requirements made by the use of the mirror in self-portraiture; or to explore their own personality and by extension find out more about the human condition generally – a quest which is at the foundation of all great portraiture. Whilst some painters may have painted just one self-portrait, others, perhaps more introspective, have created whole series.

All portraits pose a relationship between the sitter and the viewer as well as between the sitter and the artist. The viewer has the pleasure of speculating about the identity of the person in the portrait, about their life and times, and perhaps of identifying with him or her, recognizing something of himself in the picture.

Portraits can be splendid evocations of history, both on a grand or more homely scale. Details of dress, jewellery, furnishings and background help us build up a picture of the time the subject lived in. By contrast, other portraits can achieve a timeless quality by using accessories belonging not to the fashion of the day but to another bygone era. In the 18th century, for example, it was fashionable to be portrayed in a classical pose wearing garments in the antique style against a similar background. Again, some portraits are concerned with illustrating a historical or allegorical theme or situation, using an unidentified model to do so rather than concentrating on the sitter's personality or individual features.

Great portraits can be looked at again and again and yield something new on each viewing, like renewing a friendship. A portrait essentially represents a moment of truth, when a personality is captured in such a way that it tells us something about the individual sitter, ourselves and the human race all at once.

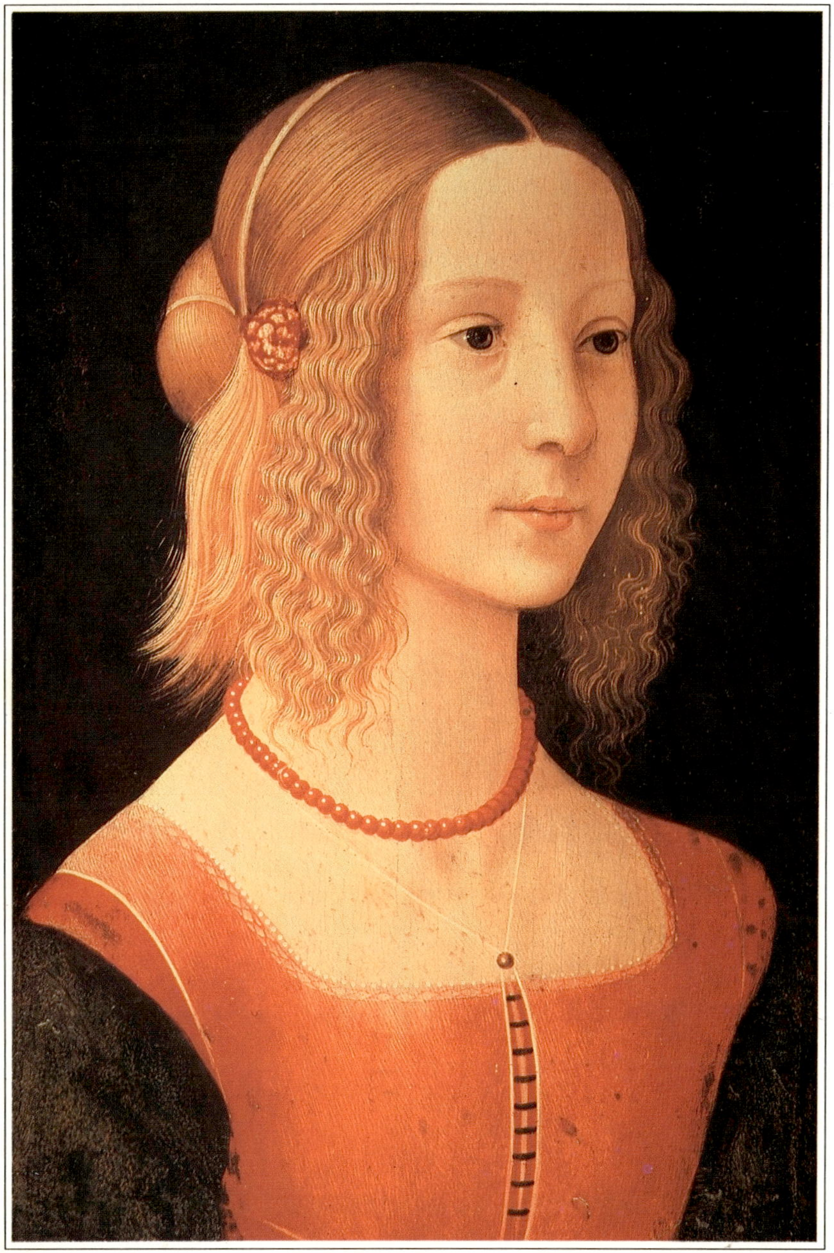

◁ **Portrait of a Girl** Domenico di Ghirlandaio (1449-94)

Oil panel

DOMENICO DI GHIRLANDAIO, born in 1449, spent his working life in Florence, the epicentre of the Renaissance in Italy, and was a consummate artist of the Quattrocento, or 1400s, the Italian term for this great flowering of artistic achievement. With his brothers Benedetto and Davide he ran a *bottega* or workshop which specialized in church decoration and also enjoyed the patronage of the affluent new middle-class clientele who were requiring family portraits as symbols of their success and status. It is likely that the young girl in this portrait, although we do not know her name, was the daughter of such a family. Although her picture was painted over 500 years ago, she is a typically fashion-conscious teenager. Her simple yet stylish scarlet dress, with its inset sleeves and scooped neckline, is matched by her red necklace and hair clasp. Her finely plucked eyebrows and elaborate hairstyle were much in vogue and feature in other portraits of the day.

▷ **Mona Lisa** Leonardo da Vinci (1452-1519)

Oil panel

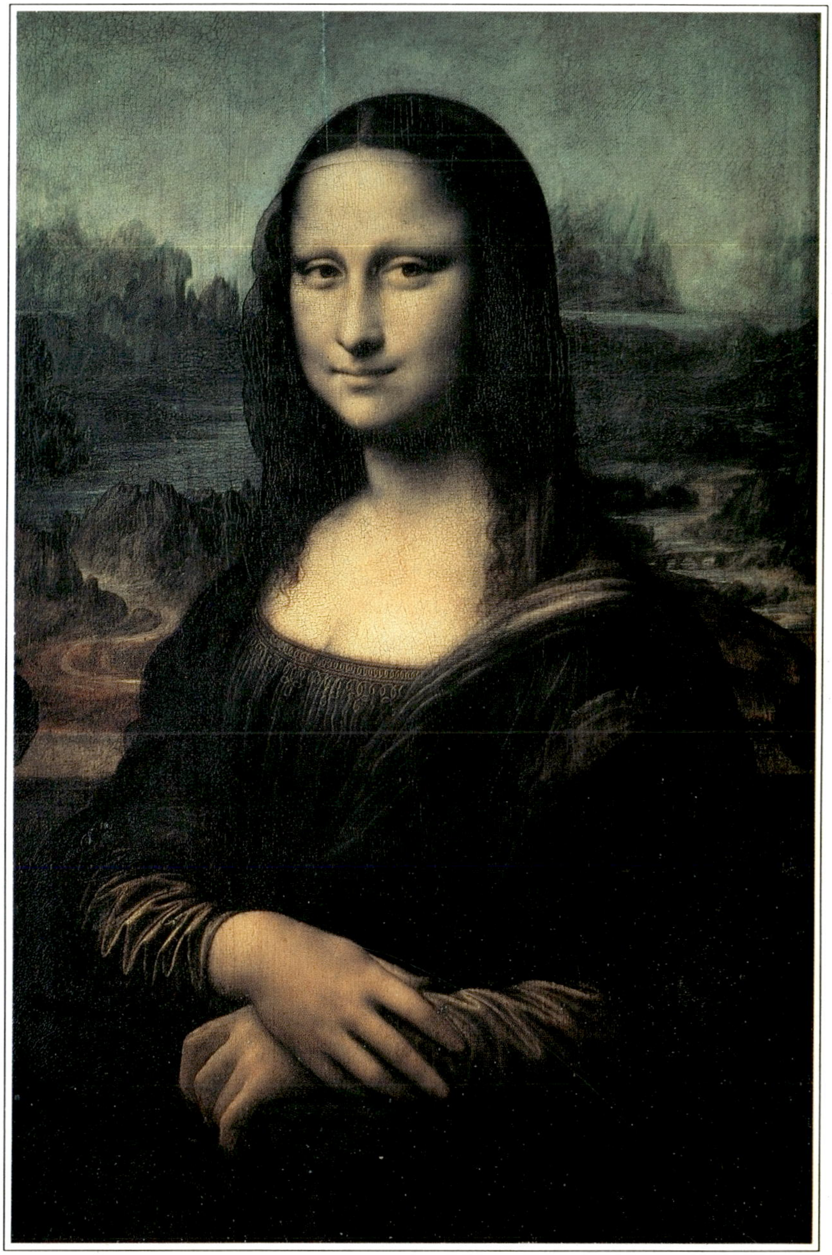

RENAISSANCE MAN and artist incarnate, Leonardo excelled as sculptor, architect, mathematician and musician as well as painter. The lady in the world's most celebrated portrait, which Leonardo finished in 1507 after working on it for four years, is Lisa Gherardini, born in 1479 and married at the age of 16 to the Florentine Francesco di Zanobi del Giocondo. *La Gioconda,* as the painting is known, is thus a pun on the subject's surname and the Italian word for cheerful, and it is indeed Mona Lisa's enigmatic, smiling expression which has made her portrait so famous. Leonardo employed musicians, singers and jesters to entertain her during sittings, which may be why she appears so relaxed, but in fact her smile, which seems so natural, may well have been a fashionable device, as recommended by contemporary books of etiquette.

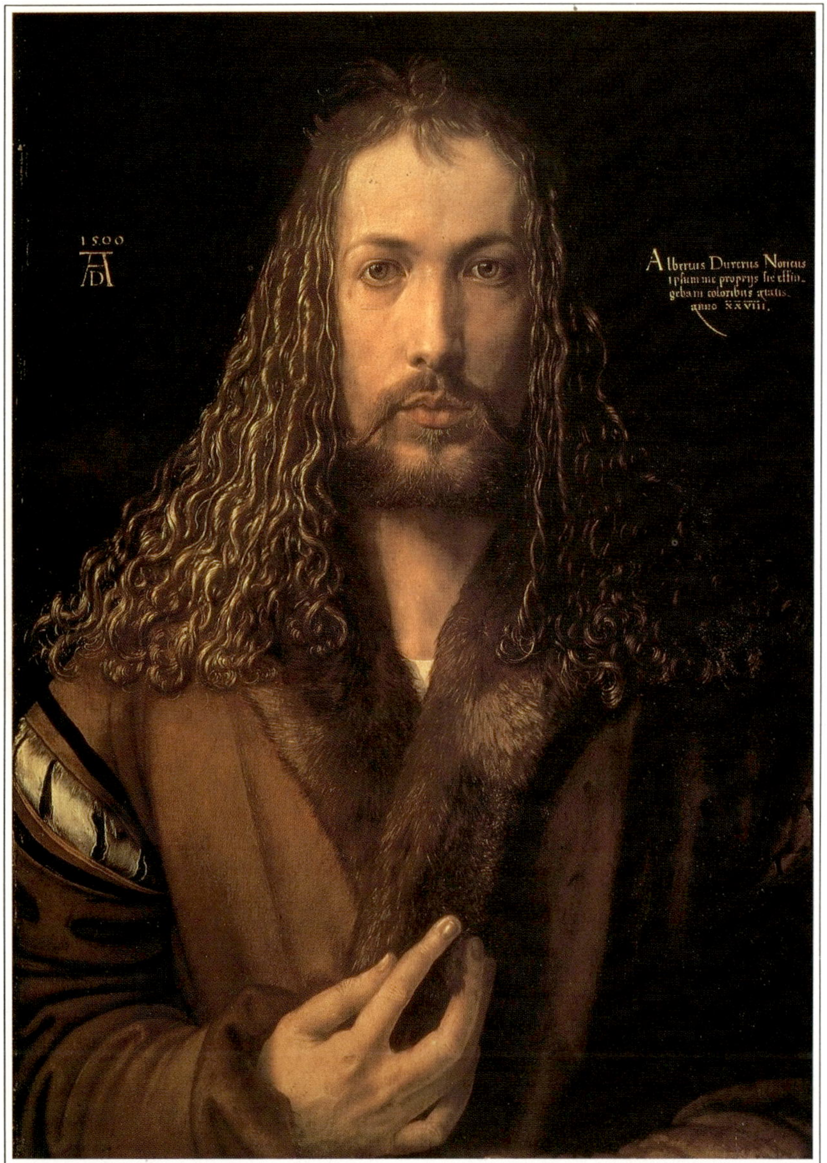

◁ **Self-portrait at the Age of 28** Albrecht Dürer (1471-1528)

Oil panel

ALBRECHT DÜRER, born in Nuremberg in Germany in 1471, was one of the greatest artists of the High Renaissance. Apprenticed at 15, he showed unusual precocity as a draughtsman, and painted a portrait of his father, who was a goldsmith, as early as 1490. He produced a number of self-portraits, one of the most famous of which, painted in 1493, the year of his engagement to Agnes Frey, shows him holding a thistle. Dürer was a man of deep religious conviction, who became an ardent follower of the Protestant reformer Martin Luther. He used himself as a model in one of his best-known paintings, *Christ as Man of Sorrows,* a terrifyingly realistic depiction of the Messiah wearing a crown of thorns. The self-portrait reproduced here is likewise suffused with religious fervour, reminiscent of the features of Christ as artists have depicted them through the ages.

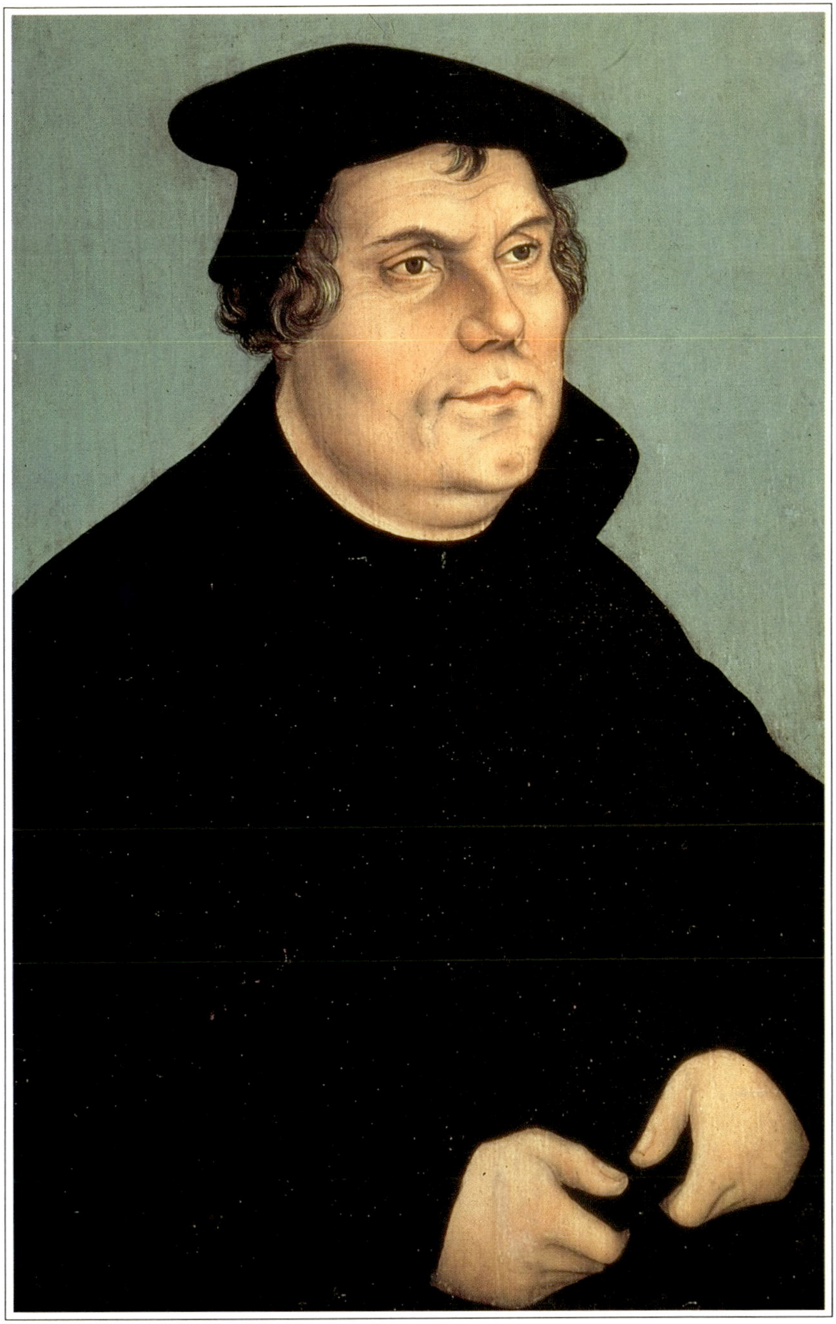

◁ **Martin Luther** Lucas Cranach the Elder (1472-1553)

Oil panel

LUCAS CRANACH THE ELDER was born in Kronach, in the Frankenwald, in 1472. He became court painter to the Electors of Saxony at Wittenberg, serving under Dukes Frederick the Wise, John the Constant and John Frederick the Magnificent. All three were enthusiasts of art (Frederick the Wise was also a patron of Dürer). Cranach enjoyed great success, and was a close friend of Martin Luther, who had nailed up the theses detailing his proposals for the Reformation in the town in 1517. Luther was godfather to Cranach's daughter Anna and Cranach in turn became godfather to Luther's first-born son, Johannes. This special relationship with its founder enabled Cranach to establish himself as chronicler of the Reformation, and it was largely through his work that the image of Luther as Reformer passed into the popular consciousness. This portrait is typical of Cranach's remarkable naturalism.

▷ **Anne of Cleves** Hans Holbein the Younger (1497/8-1543)

Oil

BORN IN AUGSBURG, Germany, Holbein took up residence in England in 1532, enjoying the patronage of Henry VIII, of whom he painted a number of striking portraits. As the King's favourite painter, he was asked to paint this portrait of Anne of Cleves, who became Henry's fourth queen following the death of Jane Seymour, although Anne's brother-in-law, Duke John of Saxony, had originally commissioned Cranach for it. Anne's father was a powerful supporter of the Reformation, which is why England's Lord Chamberlain, Thomas Cromwell, had suggested her as a suitable bride for Henry in his break with the Church of Rome. But although the marriage went ahead, Anne, who was not renowned for her looks, failed to find favour with Henry, and after only a few months it was annulled on the grounds of non-consummation. Holbein's portrait, while not exactly flattering, portrays features which are plain but pleasant enough, and what Anne lacks in beauty is compensated for by the magnificence of her attire – her ropes of precious stones, her elaborately jewelled headdress and sumptuous red velvet robe with sleeves, cuffs and neckline adorned with virginal pearls and gold filigree embroidery.

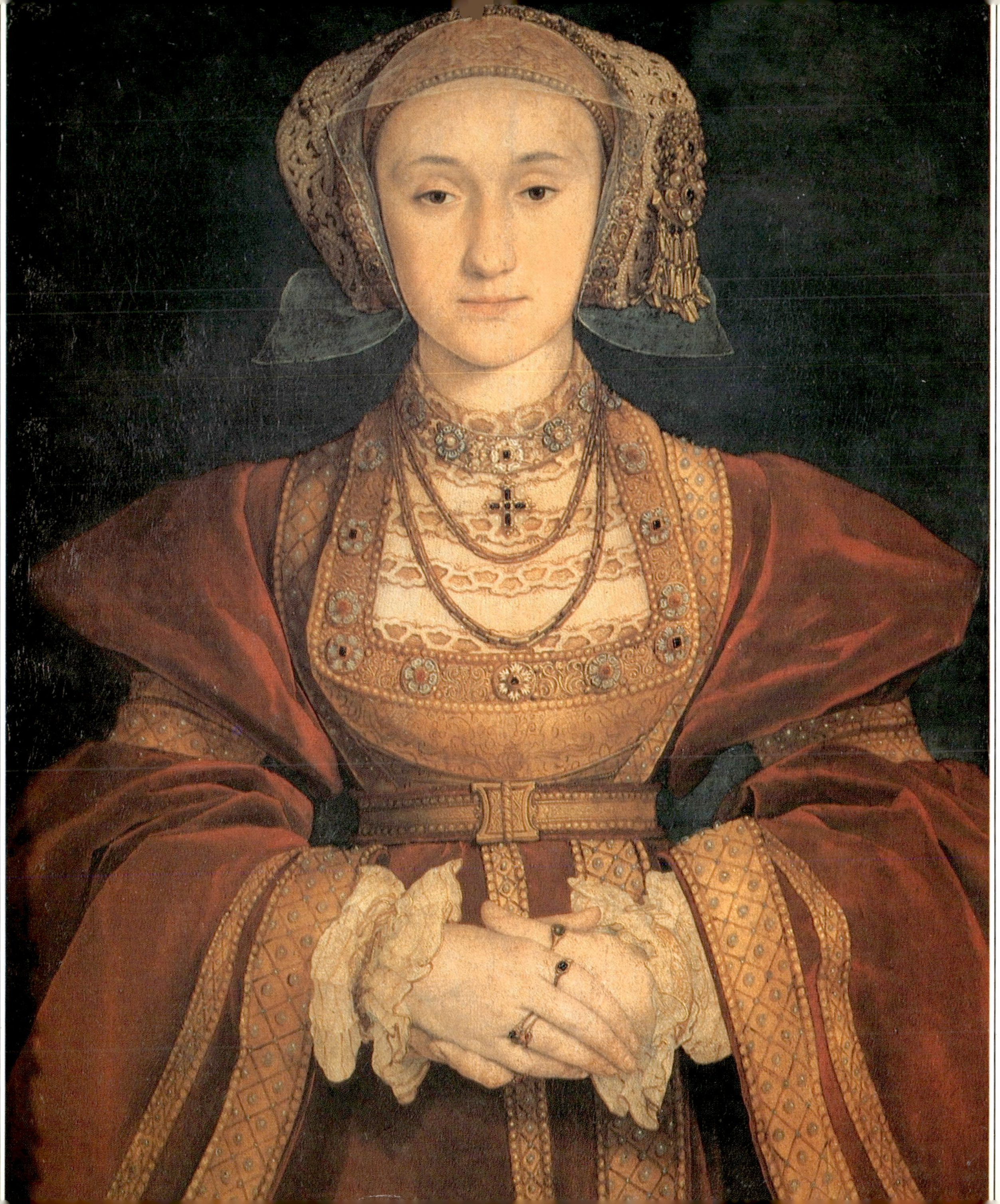

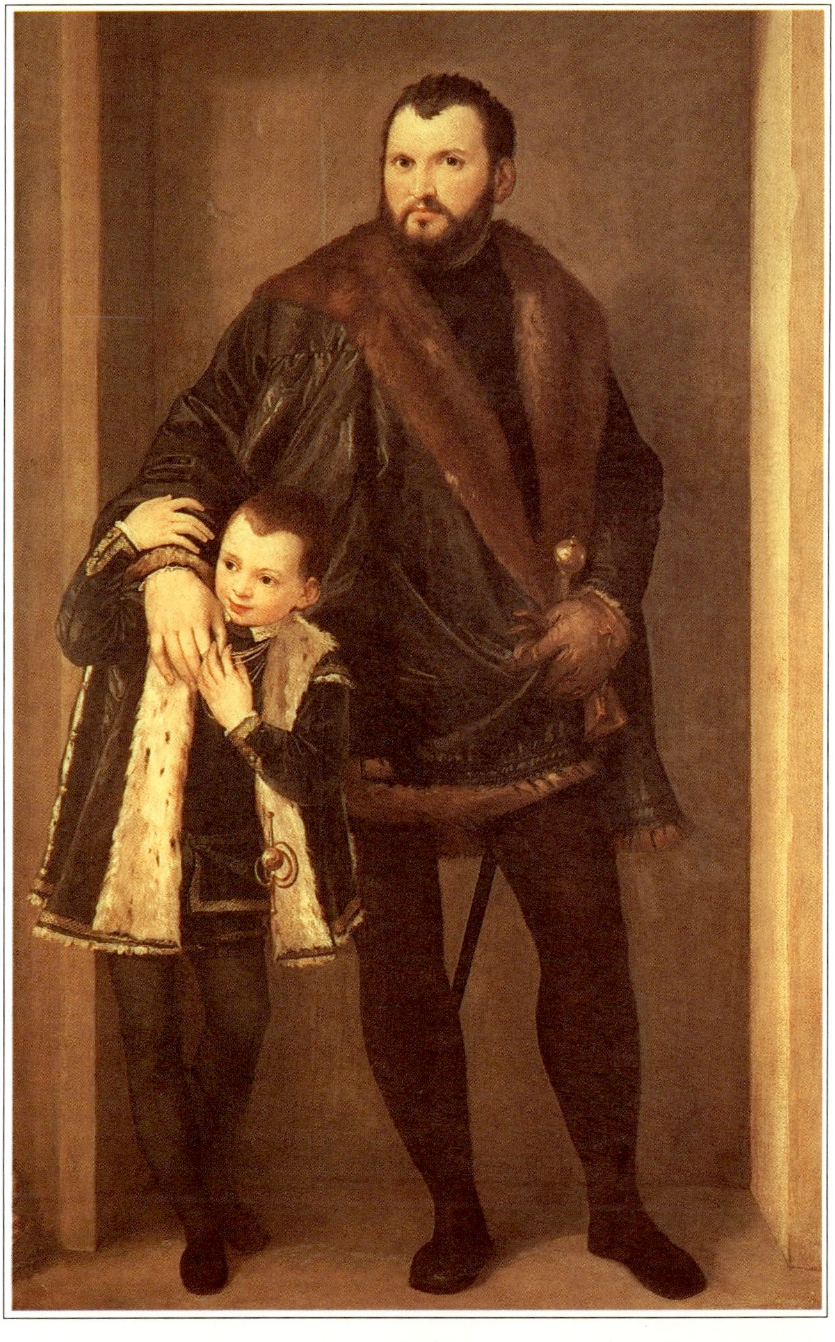

◁ **Giuseppe da Porto with his Son Antonio** Paolo Veronese (c 1528-88)

Oil

Paolo Caliari Veronese was born in Verona and later lived and worked in Venice. Although he was especially famous for his religious painting in the grand manner, he was also celebrated for his portraits and his ability to distinguish individual character behind the trappings of lineage and wealth. He was one of the great painters of children, as can be seen in this delightful study of father and son. He has brought out a marked family likeness in the similarity of their pose – each stands resting his weight on the right leg; of their dress – their cloaks are similar in cut and each is richly trimmed with fur; and of their features – both have close-cropped hair growing to a peak on the forehead. At the same time Veronese has contrasted their individual temperaments in a way that might not have been possible had he painted them separately: the father's force of character shows in the way he stares out unsmilingly at the viewer, while the lively young boy is looking to the side, as though growing restive. This double portrait is especially touching for its depiction of the affection the subjects clearly felt for each other, expressed by the closeness of their contact, the father encircling his son protectively and holding his hand, while the child places his other hand trustingly on his father's sleeve.

▷ Portrait of a Woman in a Fur Cape
El Greco (1541-1614)

Oil

DOMENIKOS THEOTOKOPOULOS was born in 1541 in Candia, Crete, and after visiting Venice and Rome between 1560 and 1570 and establishing a close association with Titian, settled in Spain, where he remained until his death in 1614. Known as 'El Greco' ('The Greek'), he enjoyed the patronage of King Philip II and is particularly famous for his paintings of religious subjects, scenes from scripture and portraits of churchmen. All his portraits, both religious and secular, have great intensity and power of suggestion, usually conveyed with sombre melancholy in a remarkably realistic way. All these qualities feature to superb effect in this outstanding portrait of an anonymous woman, a timeless embodiment of femininity. The perfect oval of the subject's face is emphasized by the plain white draped scarf. The beauty of her remarkable eyes is accentuated by means of their oblique glance.

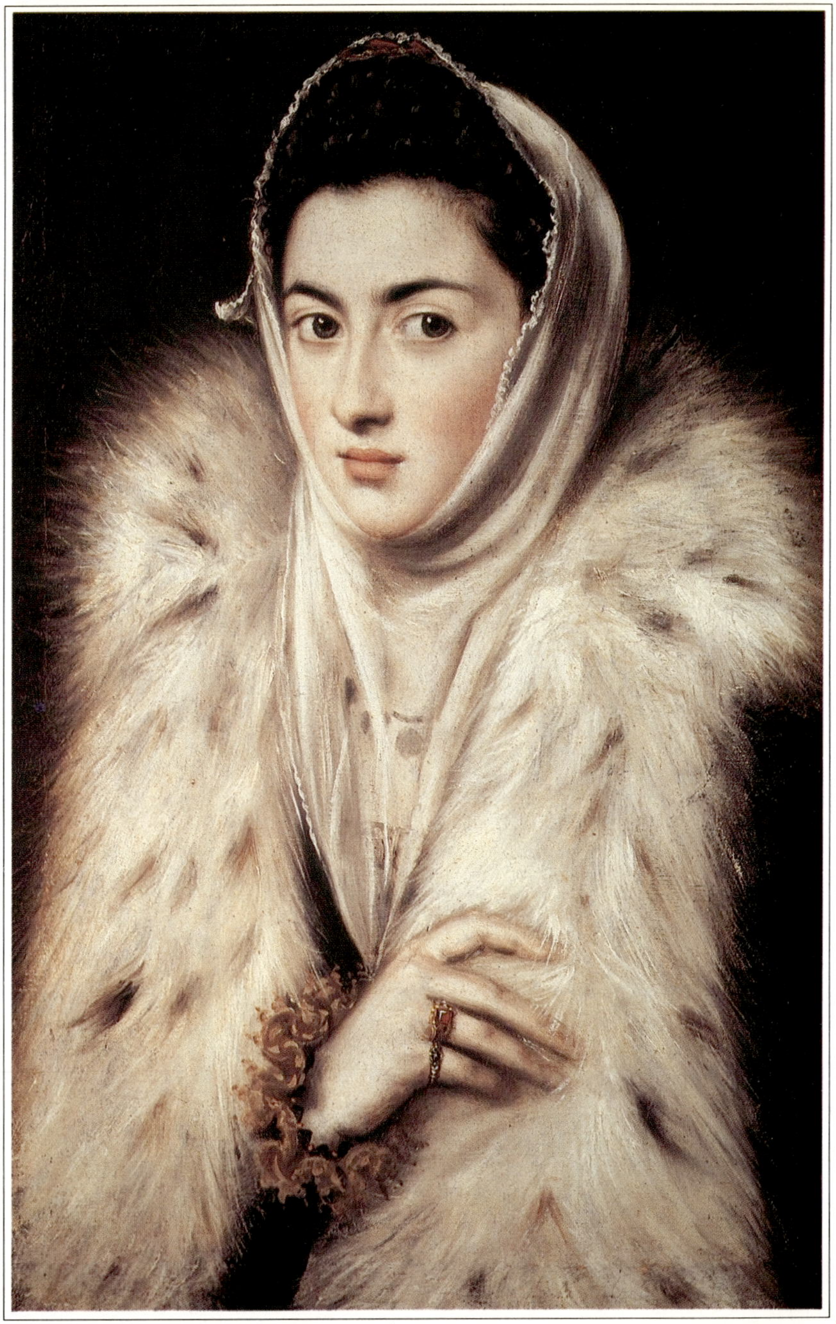

▷ **Miniature of a Young Man Against a Rose Tree** Nicholas Hilliard (1547-1619)

Watercolour on parchment

NICHOLAS HILLIARD was born in Exeter in 1547, the son of a goldsmith. He was himself apprenticed as a jeweller and goldsmith, thereby learning the skills of working in minute detail which were to serve him in such good stead for the art of miniature painting, derived from medieval manuscript illumination and called 'limning' by the Elizabethans, in which he excelled. Hilliard wrote a treatise on the subject (in which he acknowledged the influence of Holbein) and was appointed by Queen Elizabeth I, of whom and for whom he made many 'pictures in little'. The monarch much enjoyed collecting miniatures, especially of her favourites, which were worn in jewelled and enamelled lockets. The miniature reproduced here, which was painted in 1588, the year of England's defeat of the Armada, measures only 6 x 5 cm (2 $^{3}/_{8}$ x 2 ins). The identity of the subject in this painting is unknown.

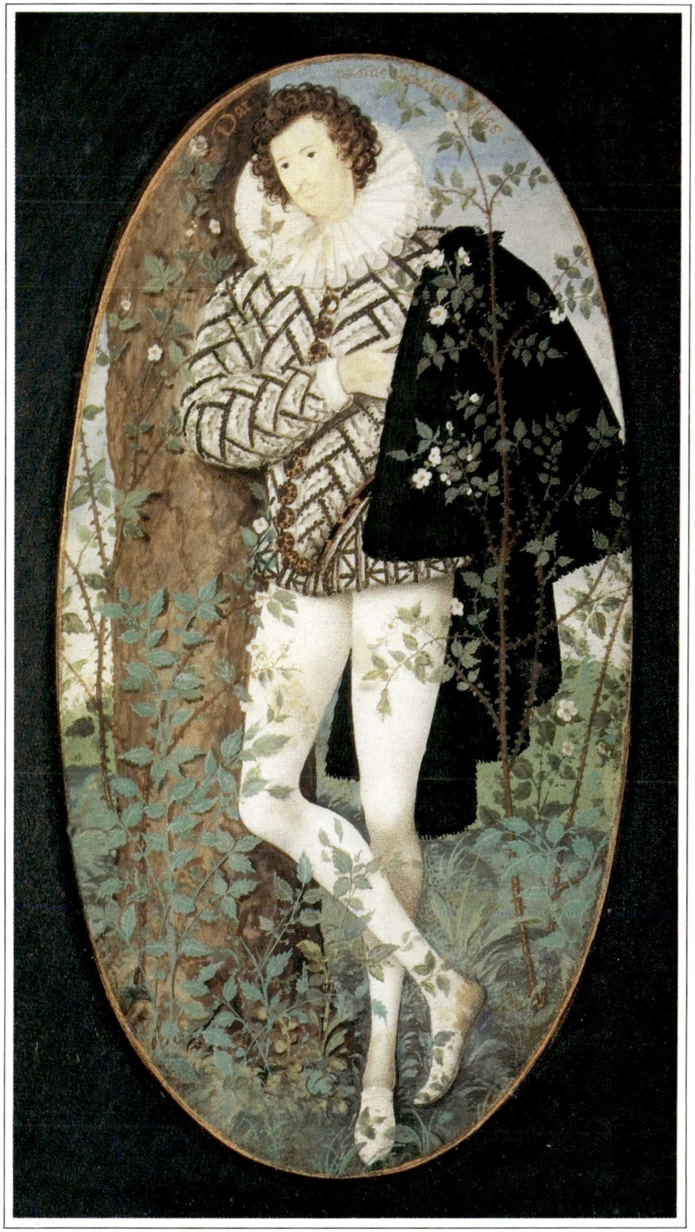

▷ **Queen Elizabeth I** Marcus Gheeraerts the Younger (c 1561-1635)

Oil

BROTHER-IN-LAW of the Huguenot-born Isaac Oliver, star pupil of the miniaturist Nicholas Hilliard, Gheeraerts was one of the many – often unknown – artists to paint Elizabeth I. This remarkable woman, whose childhood as the daughter of the disgraced and beheaded Anne Boleyn was a long lesson in survival, came to the throne in 1558 and proved herself the true child of Henry VIII (although it was often rumoured she was a bastard) by the shrewd and dedicated way in which she restored unity to her country and made England a world power. There is something of her father's expression in the Queen's pursed lips and uncompromising gaze in this portrait. Elizabeth never married, instead playing off her suitors against each other and retaining her cherished image as Virgin Queen, and the vanity that went with it, into old age. In this portrait she is well into her fifties, yet her magnificent silver gauze ruff and silvery white dress proclaim her virginity. Her love of jewels, especially pearls, is evident in their lavish use and intricate portrayal on her dress, in her ears, round her neck and in her hair – which is of course a wig. Her pale complexion testifies to the skills of her ladies-in-waiting, who took immense pains with their royal mistress's make-up.

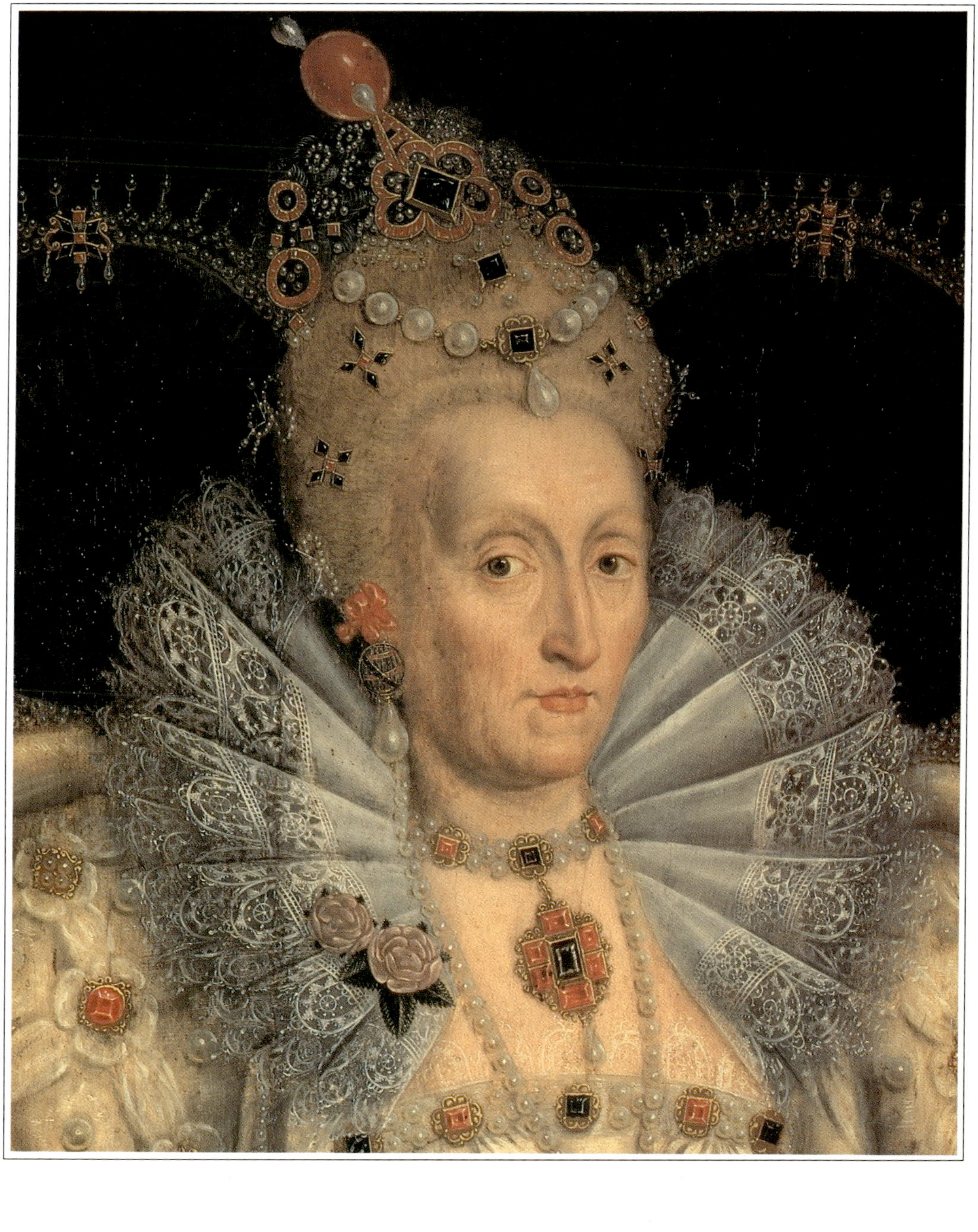

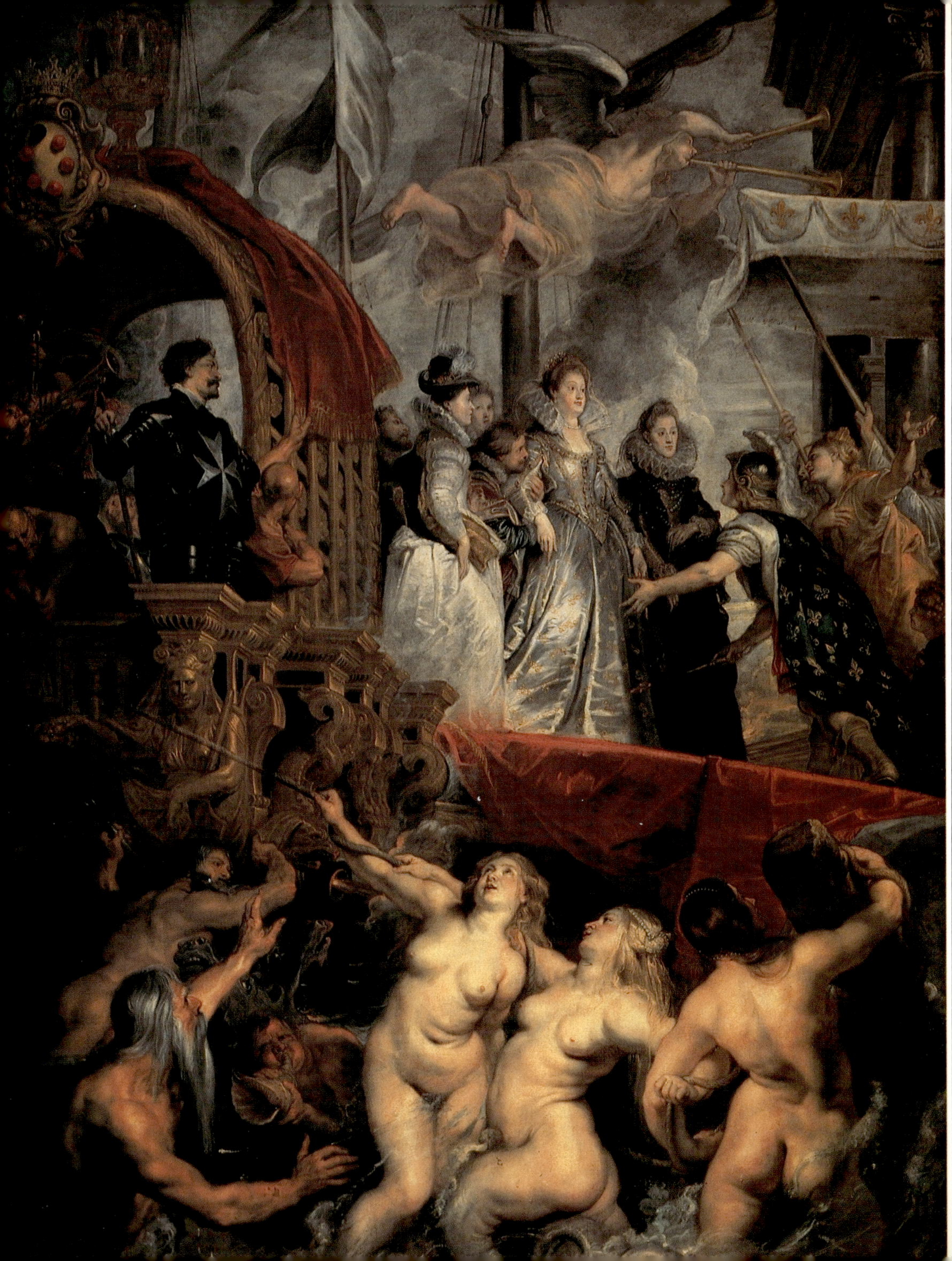

◁ **The Arrival of Marie de Medici in Marseilles** Peter Paul Rubens (1577-1640)

Oil

RUBENS, THE FLEMISH MASTER born in 1577, was the creator of the baroque style in painting, giving powerful, dynamic expression to historical and mythological themes. The style is perfectly illustrated in this dramatic picture, the fifth in a series commissioned by the Florentine-born Marie de Medici, mother of Louis XIII and Dowager Queen of France, to adorn the walls of the Luxembourg Palace which she had built to commemorate her return to Paris after being temporarily banished by her son. The series of 21 paintings celebrating Marie's virtues and achievements presented no easy task, for in reality the Queen was self-centred, foolish and quarrelsome, and no beauty. But Rubens succeeded brilliantly by mixing allegory with realism, and completed the series in three years, from 1622 to 1625. Each painting is an extended portrait of Marie as the focal point; here she is depicted arriving in the port of Marseilles from Italy, prior to her marriage to Henri IV. Escorted by an elaborately dressed courtier and solicitous lady-in-waiting, Marie is presented allegorically amidst the gods of Olympus, conveyed by Father Neptune and a trio of voluptuous water nymphs, greeted by the helmeted figure of France and heralded by the flying goddess of Fame.

▷ **Las Meniñas** Diego Velazquez (1599-1660)

Oil panel

THE SPANISH PAINTER Velazquez, born in Seville in 1599, was one of the greatest portraitists. He was fond of domestic themes and early in his career often chose low-life models. From the 1620s, when he became official painter to the court of Philip IV, his style became of necessity more dignified, but he still loved to introduce a note of informality, and never to greater effect than in this ingenious and witty masterpiece painted in 1656. It is a portrait within a portrait and an early example of the conversation piece or informal group portrait, in this case involving the Spanish royal family. The Infanta Margarita, daughter of Philip IV and his second wife (and niece) Maria-Anna of Austria, is the central, principal figure. Velazquez painted more formal individual portraits of the Infanta, but here she is shown in a brilliantly captured real-life moment, visiting the studio where Velazquez is painting her parents. Together with her maids of honour (the *meniñas,* or young girls, of the title), her court dwarfs and a dog, she is looking eagerly out of the picture to where the King and Queen are posing, unseen except in their reflection in the mirror at the far end of the room. Velazquez stands at his easel, intent on his subject.

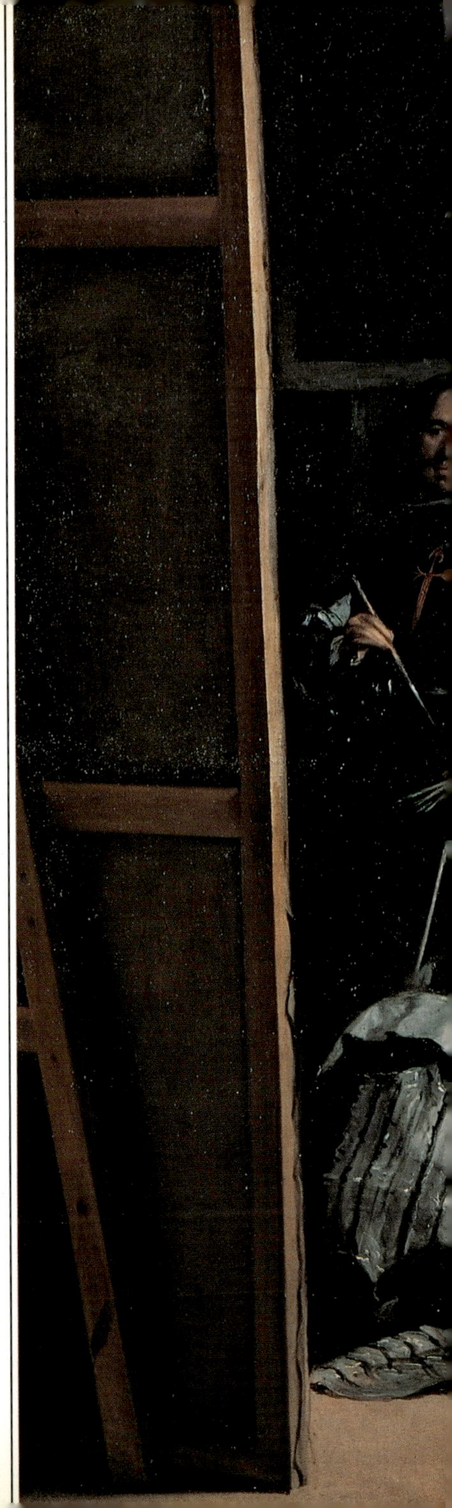

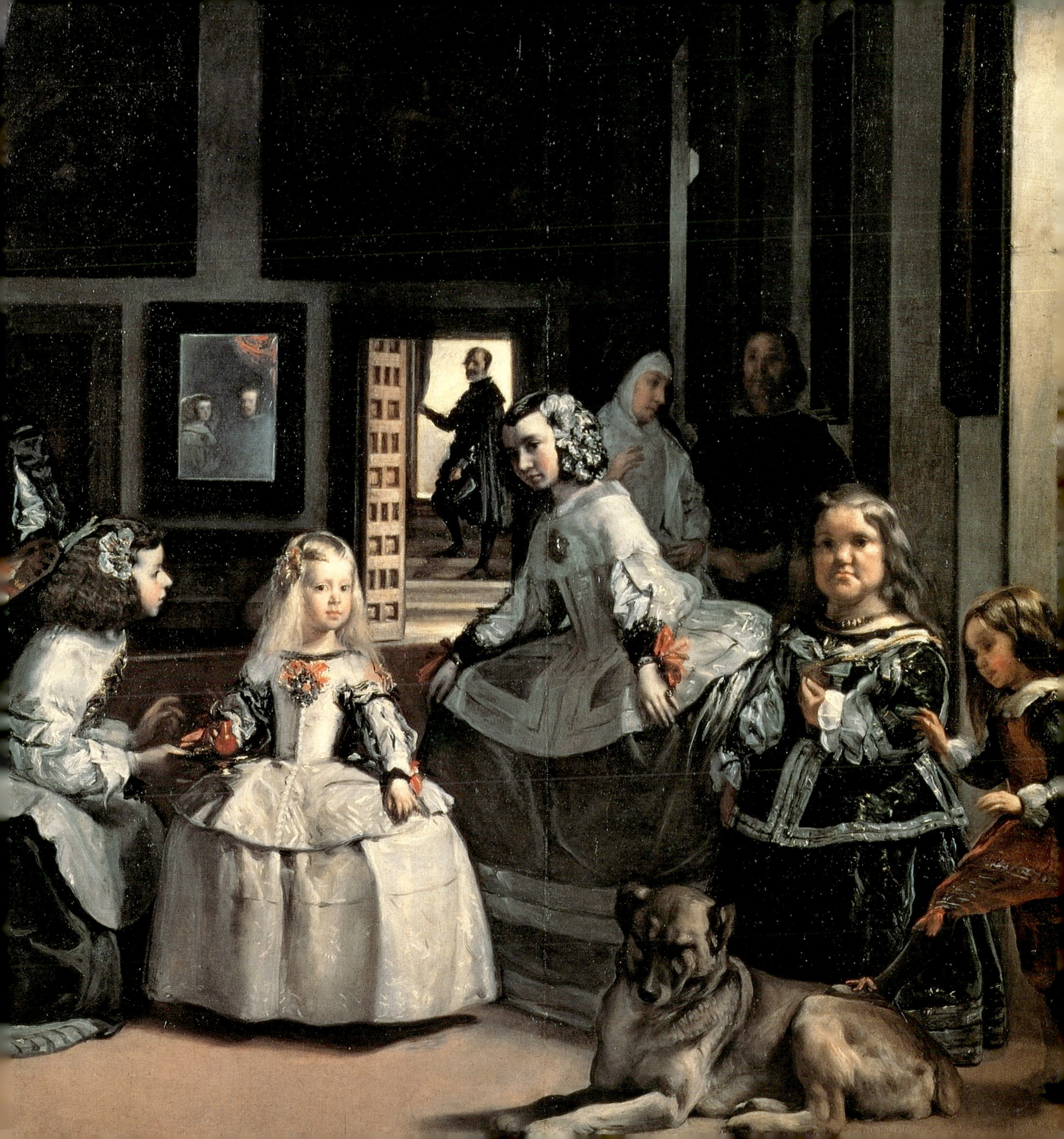

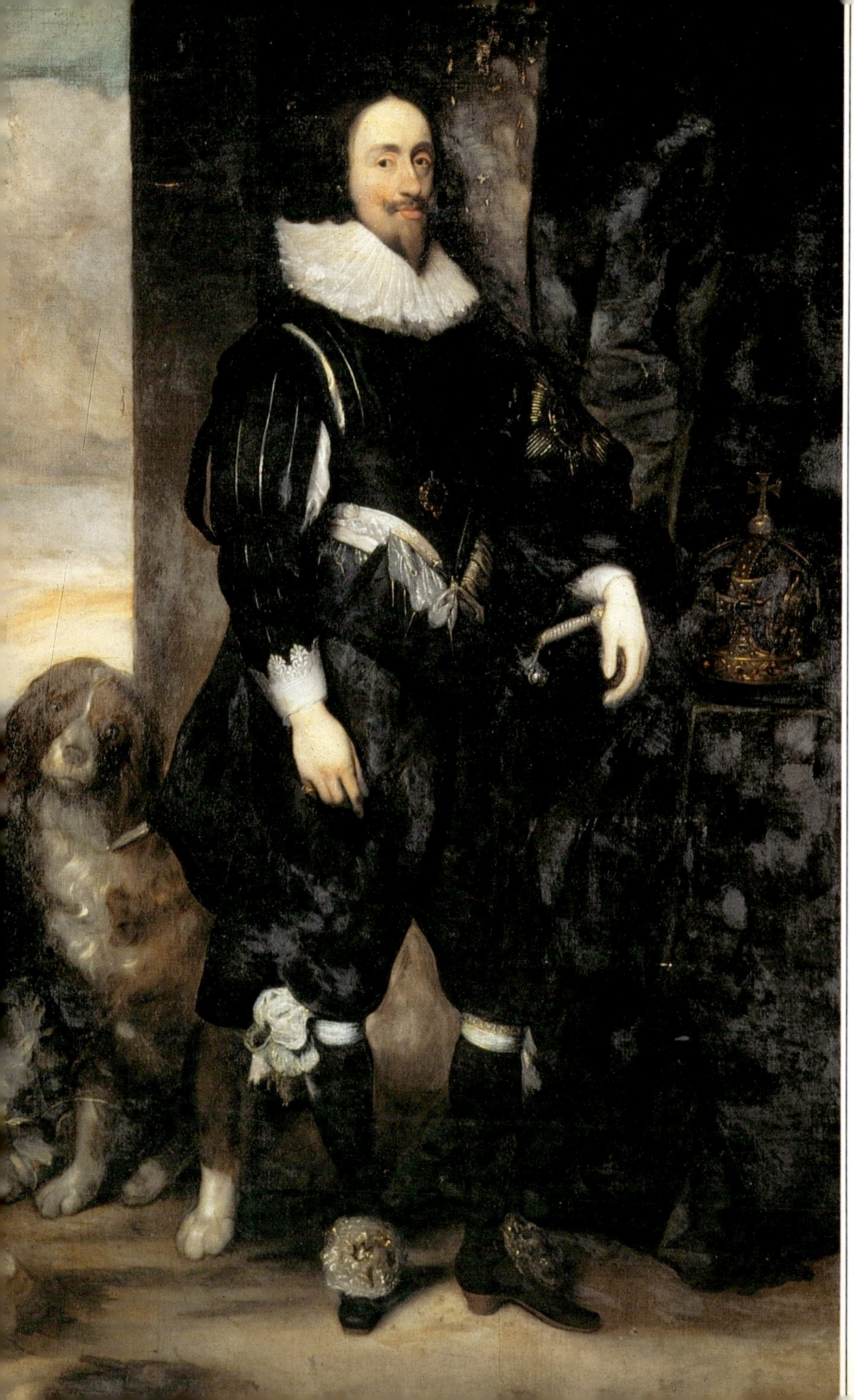

◁ **King Charles I wearing the Order of the Garter**
Sir Anthony van Dyck (1599-1641)

Oil

BORN IN 1599, van Dyck worked with Rubens before first visiting England at the age of 21. It was not until 1632, however, that he became chief painter to Charles I (1600-49). The King, who was passionately interested in the arts, was a serious collector. He regarded van Dyck as heir to Titian and in July 1632 conferred on him a knighthood and a substantial pension. In return van Dyck painted members of the court and the royal family over a seven-year period. He had a lifelong fascination with court life. This portrait shows Charles majestically attired in his Garter robes, the picture of restrained sartorial elegance and the simple dignity symbolized by the Order of the Garter. The King's sombre look was characteristic – he had a serious, melancholy disposition. Beside him stands the royal crown as an emblem of majesty.

▷ **Self-portrait in Fancy Dress**
Rembrandt (1606-69)

Oil

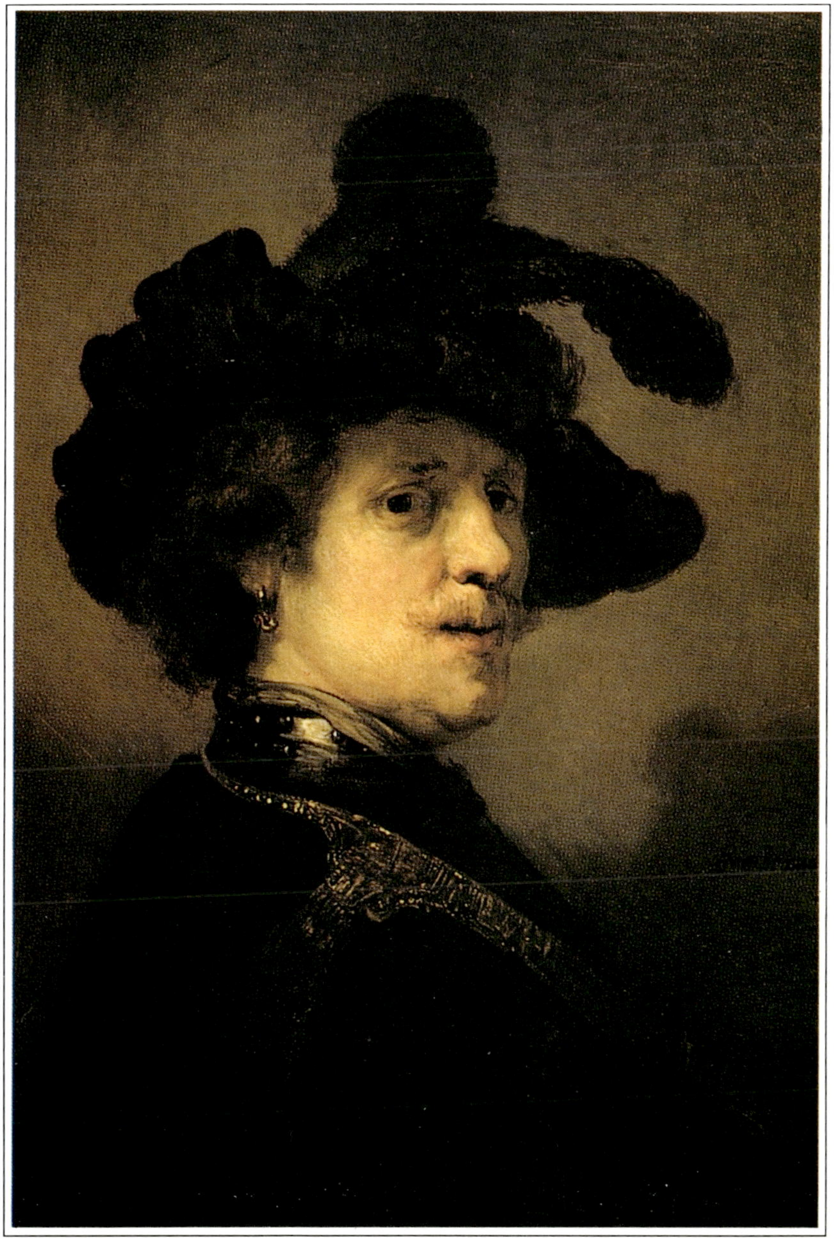

REMBRANDT VAN RIJN established himself as a portrait painter in Amsterdam in the early 1630s and produced some of the most superb portraits in the history of painting, always remarkably lifelike. Being a prolific painter (there are some 650 works by him), Rembrandt created a whole gallery of faces. He also produced a unique series of self-portraits, some 90 in all, including drawings and etchings as well as paintings. Many artists have painted themselves, and of course any self-portrait provides a fascinating glimpse into an artist's personality and how he saw himself. But in Rembrandt's case his self-portraits form a complete autobiography from the age of 21 to 63, and because of the depth and range of his vision they seem to represent the whole course of human life, from youth through maturity to old age. Rembrandt was a carefree 30 when he painted this flamboyant, light-hearted portrait of himself in fancy dress.

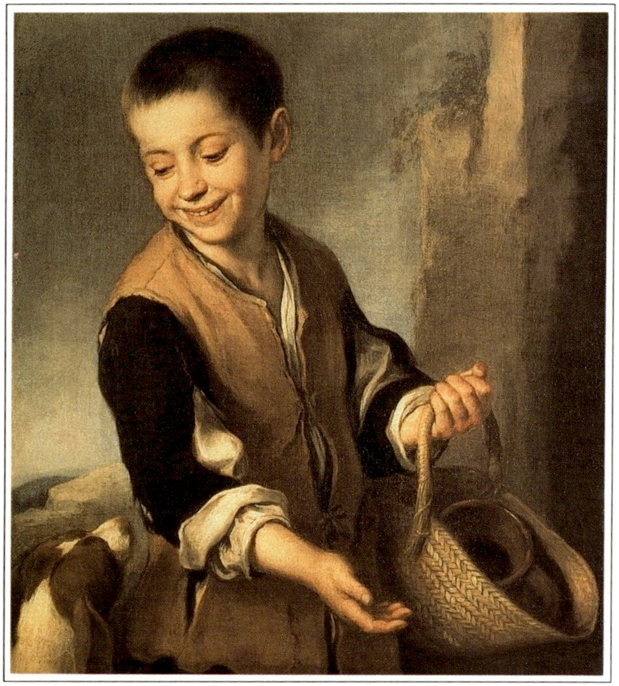

△ **Boy with a Dog** Bartolome Murillo (1617-82)

Oil

MURILLO, born in Seville in 1617, became most famous for his religious paintings, but all his work, sacred and secular, is marked by a blend of realism and sentiment. Murillo had a great love for children and a quite remarkable ability to capture the innocence of childhood: he used the street urchins of his native Andalusia as his models in a way that was quite unprecedented at the time. The wide grin of the boy looking lovingly at the dog in this portrait expresses his involvement and delight in the simple things that matter so much in childhood – in this case an animal. The child is holding a basket containing a ceramic vessel, as though he has been sent on an errand but has got distracted on the way, like children the world over.

▷ **Portrait of a Lady, said to be Nell Gwynn**
Sir Peter Lely (1618-80)

Oil on canvas

LELY WAS OF Dutch parentage – his real name was Pieter van der Faes. He came to London in the 1640s, shortly after the death of van Dyck, by whom he was influenced. Lely in turn became one of the most influential painters of the 17th century. Although his portraits have marked resemblances to each other, almost as though they were of members of the same family, and not necessarily, one suspects, altogether accurate likenesses of the sitters, Lely captured to perfection the mood of languid sensuality which prevailed at Charles II's pleasure-loving Restoration court. He became Principal Painter to the King in 1661 and established a large studio of assistants. This painting, believed to be of Charles II's mistress, Nell Gwynn, is a studio work. It contains no hint of Nell's orange-selling days – instead she is portrayed as a typical Restoration lady.

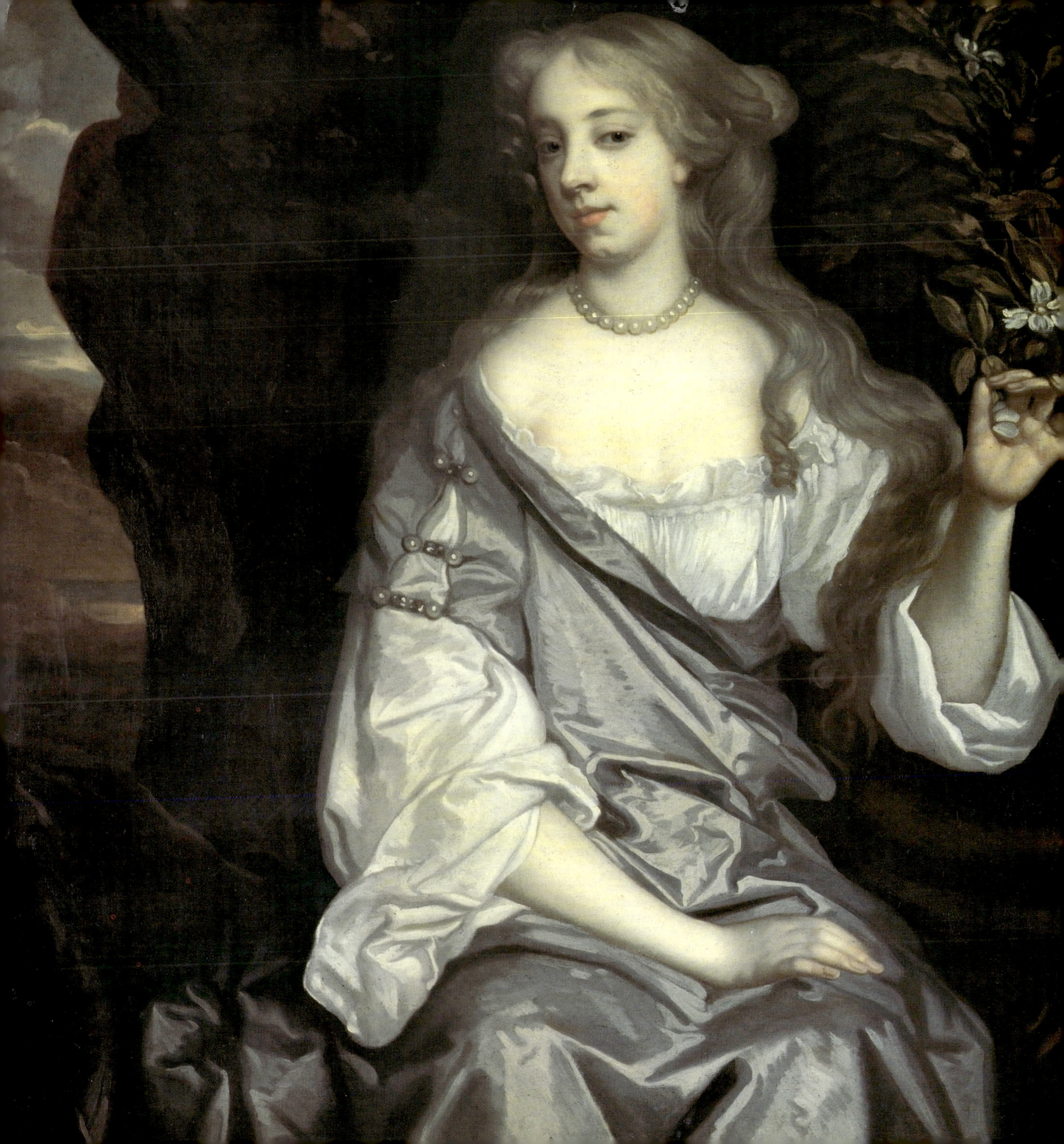

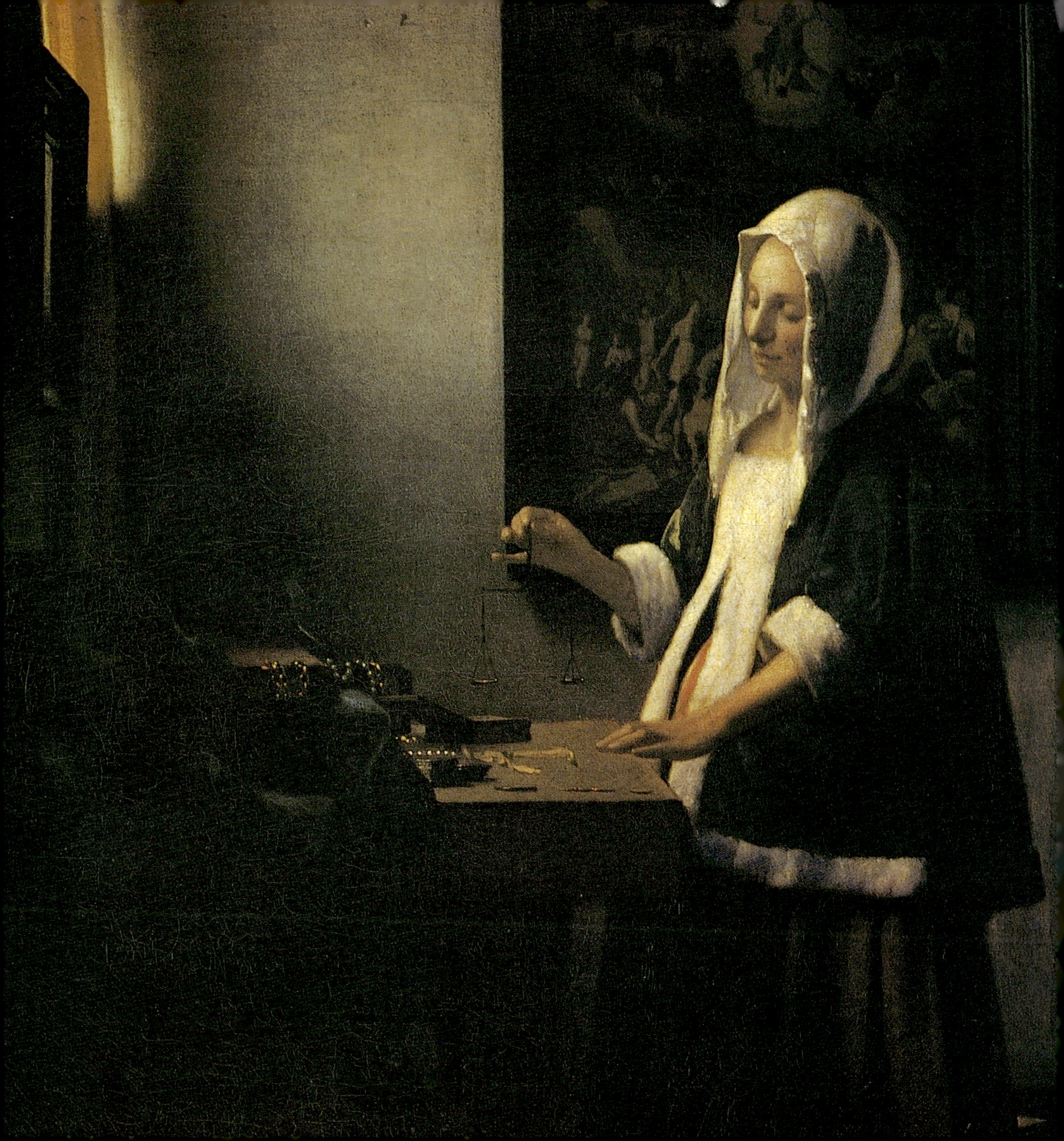

◁ **Woman Weighing Gold**
Jan Vermeer (1632-75)

Oil

VERMEER, who was born in Delft, Holland, in 1632 and died there at the age of 43, was one of the greatest 17th-century Dutch painters to specialize in domestic interiors. Very little is known of his life, but he must certainly have worked very slowly and painstakingly, for only 40 paintings by him are known. A sense of peace and calm is characteristic of his work; he liked to show his figures preoccupied with some everyday task, such as housework, writing or playing a musical instrument, in a serene, orderly, domestic setting. As Vermeer's subjects are portrayed totally involved in an absorbing activity there is no element whatsoever of self-consciousness on their part. Here the woman is so engrossed in the business of weighing the gold on the balance scales in front of her she appears quite unaware that she is being painted. The simplicity of structure and its interplay of shadow and light are typical of Vermeer.

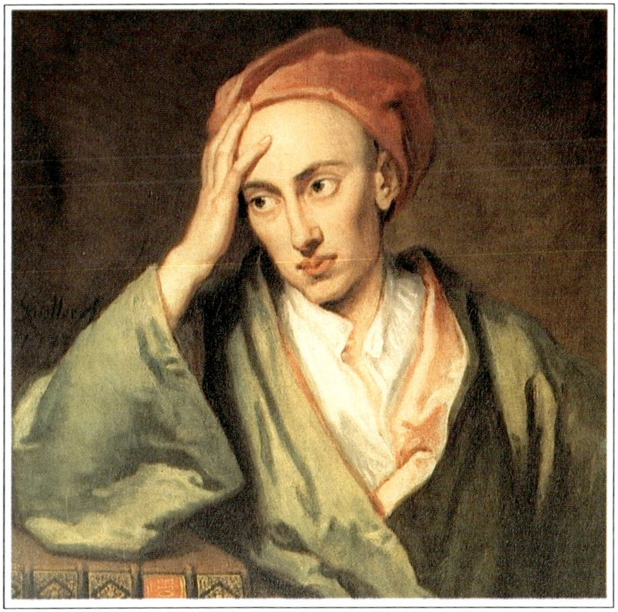

△ **Alexander Pope** Sir Godfrey Kneller (1646-1723)

Oil on canvas

LIKE SIR PETER LELY, Kneller was born in Germany – his name was originally Gottfried Kniller. Like Lely, too, he became official painter to the English royal court, and in 1680 was granted a baronetcy by George I. Kneller was the last in a distinguished line of immigrant court painters in England, descending from Holbein through van Dyck. Also like his predecessor Sir Peter Lely, he directed a vast studio which produced literally thousands of portraits. His portrait of Alexander Pope (1688-1744) at the age of 34 shows him seated rather than standing, for the poet, who was deformed, was only 1.37 m (4 ft 6 ins) in height. Pope, best known for his epic satires, *The Rape of the Lock* and *The Dunciad,* was also a brilliant translator of Greek epic poetry, so is posed with his right elbow leaning on a volume of Homer.

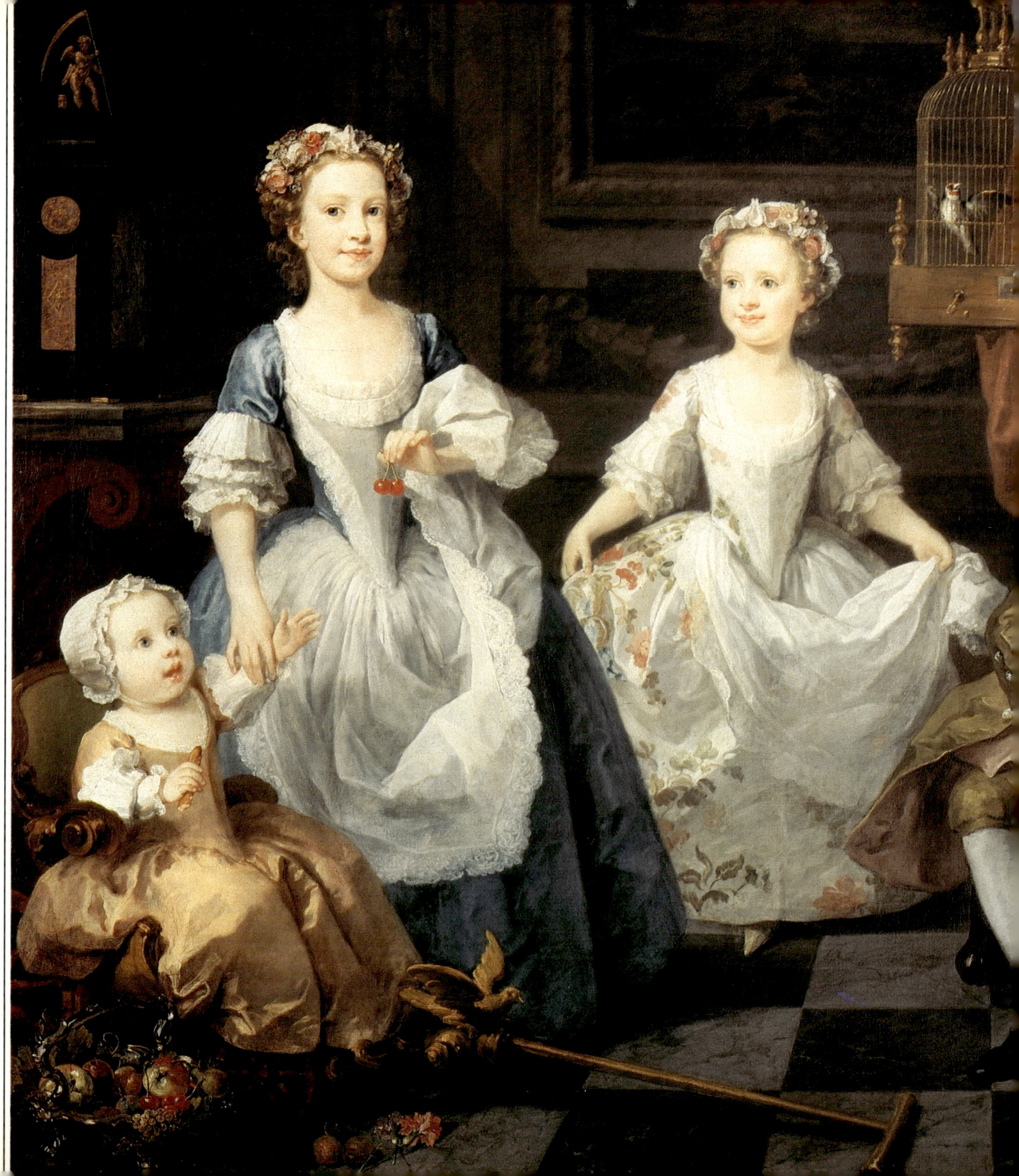

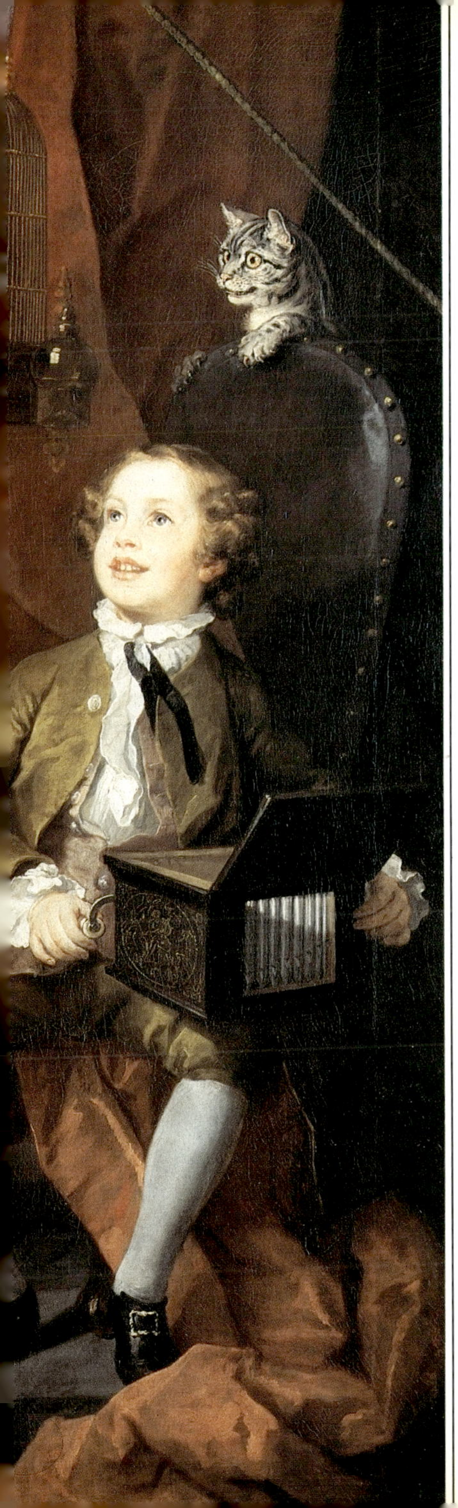

◁ **The Graham Children** William Hogarth (1697-1764)

Oil on canvas

HOGARTH, born in London in 1697, was the liveliest of portrait painters. His conversation pieces, showing members of a family involved in customary routines and diversions, are particularly remarkable for their animation. Conversation pieces are especially attractive and entertaining because of their sense of intimacy – in contrast with stiff, set-piece portraits they are more like informal snapshots, showing people at ease in a familiar environment. Hogarth, a master of the genre, was able to bring out fully different personalities, as in this portrait of the children of Daniel Graham, apothecary to the Royal Hospital, Chelsea. The children's parents do not make an appearance: for this reason, perhaps, the Graham boy is portrayed in particularly exuberant mood, while his eldest sister, wearing an apron, seems to be playing the role of mother, solemnly holding the toddler's hand and dangling a cluster of cherries to amuse her. Her younger sister, on the other hand, appears entranced by what must have been her best dress, totally oblivious to anything else. The picture is full of symbolic images, contributing to its charm: a figure of Time bearing a scythe on the clock represents the fleeting nature of youth; there is a picture of Orpheus charming the beasts on the side of the hand organ, but the Graham family cat, perched on the back of the chair, seems about to strike at the bird in its gilded cage.

▷ **A Young Man Drawing**
Jean-Baptiste Chardin
(1699-1779)

Oil on canvas

CHARDIN WAS BORN in Paris in 1699, the son of a cabinet-maker. He excelled in the art of still-life and is probably best remembered for his intriguing studies of musical instruments, fruit, game and kitchen pots and pans. He was also a fine portraitist and master of genre scenes, showing people involved in a variety of activities and pastimes: getting dressed, saying grace, learning to write, drawing water, embroidering, blowing bubbles, playing with a top, building a house of cards, and so on. Just as people took pleasure in identifying with Chardin's homely still-lifes, they enjoyed his intimate scenes of daily life in the same way. Through the sheer quality of his painting he elevated even the most down-to-earth scenes and mundane actions into something timeless and beautiful.

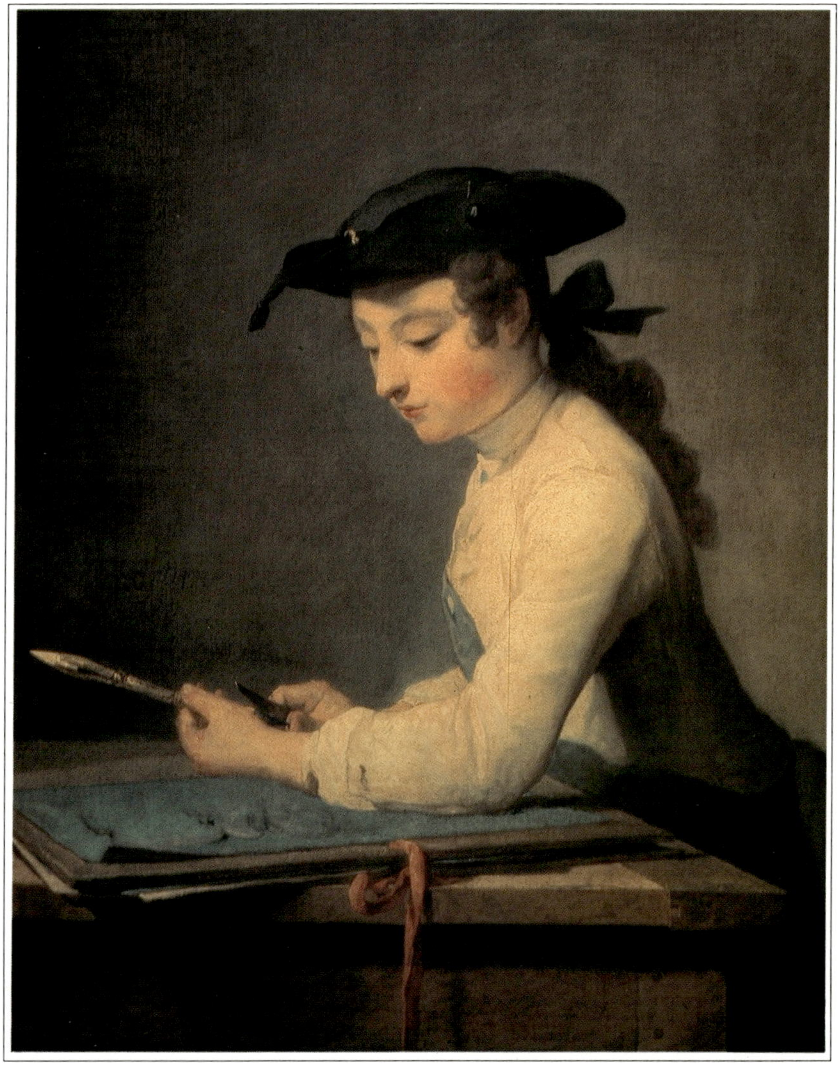

▷ **Louis XV in Coronation Robes** Hyacinthe Rigaud (1659–1743)

Oil on canvas

RIGAUD, BORN IN Perpignan in 1659, went to Paris in 1681 and became official court painter and distinguished portraitist of Louis XIV. Strongly influenced by van Dyck's vision of majesty, Rigaud worked almost exclusively at court, also serving the Sun King's great-grandson and successor, Louis XV. His paintings epitomize baroque state portraiture at its height, a quality most apparent in this fine portrait of the boy-king Louis XV, who succeeded in 1715 to the French monarchy at the age of 5 (like his great-grandfather before him), but was not formally crowned until the grand old age of 13! The young king was immensely popular with his subjects, and Rigaud has made the most of his natural good looks. All the trappings of majesty are there, from the sceptre and magnificent coronation robes to the state throne upholstered with the fleur-de-lys of France.

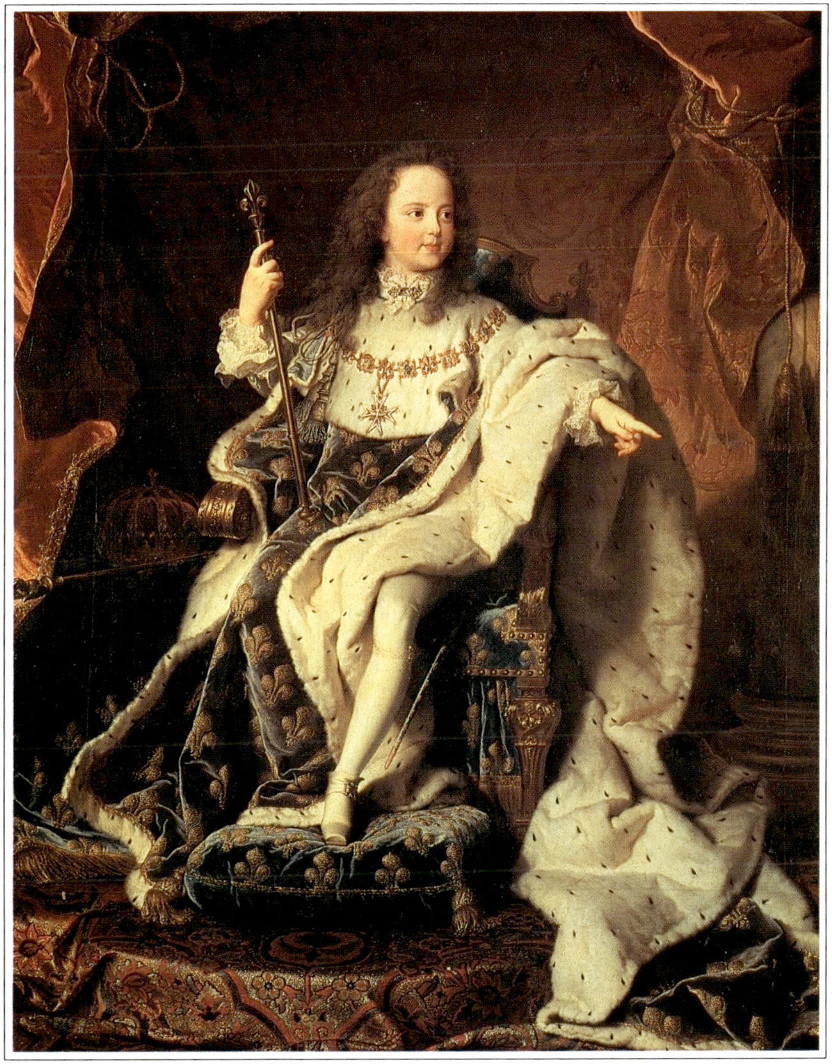

▷ Sir John Nelthorpe Shooting with Two Pointers
George Stubbs (1724-1806)

Oil on canvas

STUBBS, BORN IN Liverpool in 1724, is most famous for his equestrian portraits (the son of a currier, he became an expert in anatomy). He excelled not only in catering to the English love of hunting and racing, but also in portraying the life-style of the landed classes in sporting conversation pieces like the portrait reproduced here. The Nelthorpes of Scawby, Lincolnshire, were Stubbs's first recorded patrons, and he had painted John Nelthorpe at the age of 10 some 20 years before the present portrait in 1776.

The painting illustrates superbly the English attachment to country life pursuits and also a sense of the power of the landowner, conveyed through both the determined features and commanding stance of Sir John, who succeeded his father, Sir Henry, as 8th baronet, and the sweep of the land belonging to him in the background. The setting is Barton Fields on the Nelthorpe estate, with the village of Barton-upon-Humber and the river estuary behind.

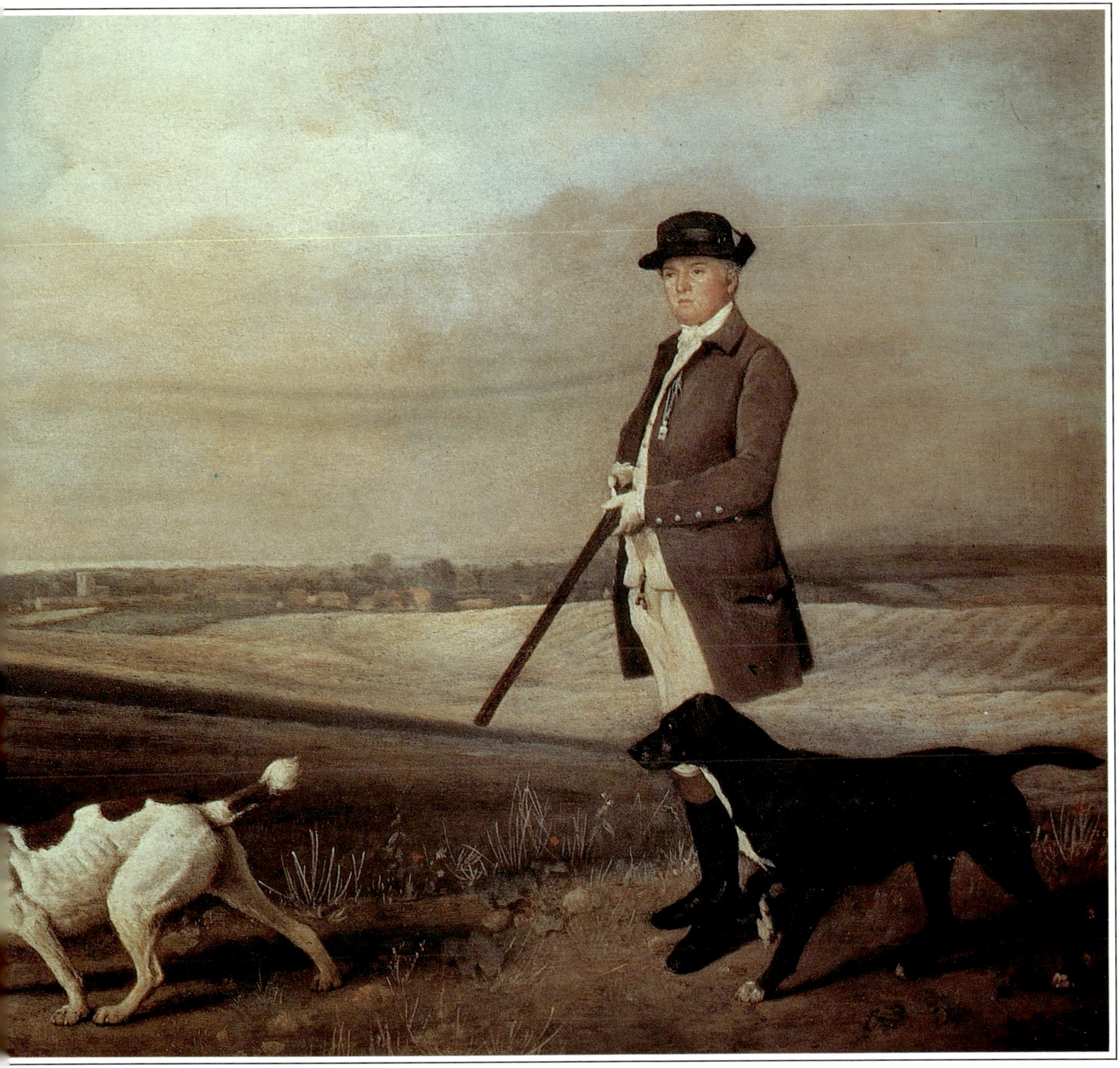

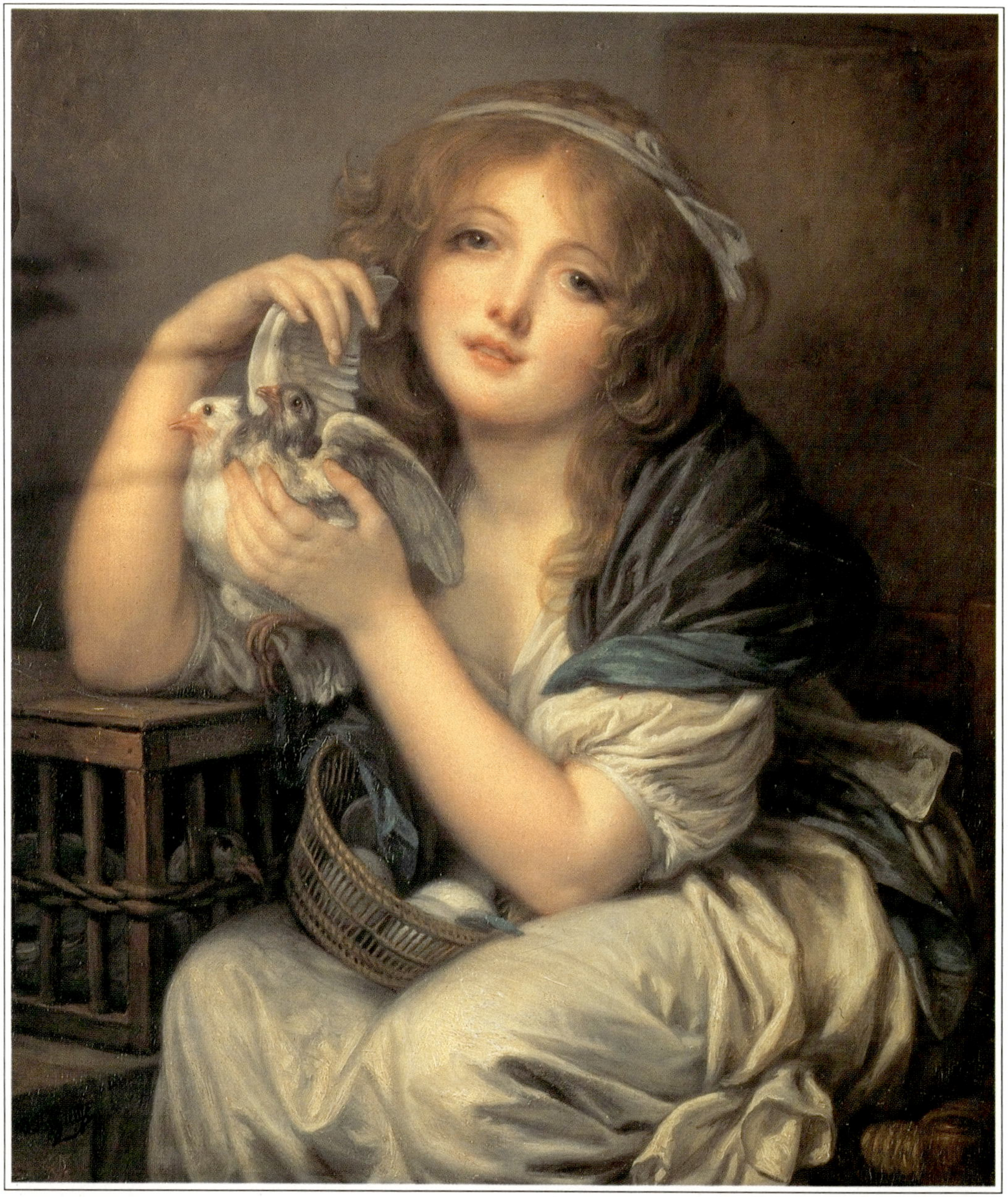

◁ **Girl with Doves** Jean-Baptiste Greuze (1725-1805)

Oil on canvas

GREUZE, BORN IN 1725 in Tournus (near Mâcon), France, where there is today a Musée Greuze, made his name with narrative genre paintings like *A Grandfather Reading the Bible to His Family* and *The Paralytic Tended by His Children,* extolling the rewards of simple virtue. He enjoyed a meteoric rise to fame in 1755 following his first exhibition at the Salon de Paris, and his success seems to have gone to his head, for fellow-artists found his conceit unbearable. Greuze was especially popular for his 'Expression Studies', such as *The Dreamer* and *Girl Weeping over Her Dead Bird.* The *Girl with Doves – L'Innocence Tenant Deux Pigeons* in French – is one such. The cloying sentimentality of the subject is only prevented from becoming mawkish by the freshness and lightness of touch in the painting. Blue and white are of course the colours of innocence, and a basket of eggs lies in the girl's lap while she gently cups the doves with one hand and caresses their wings with the other. The innocence of the subject's tender pose, candid glance and trembling lower lip is underlined by an element of sensual voluptuousness which is characteristic of Greuze's work.

▷ David Garrick as Sir John Brute in Vanbrugh's *The Provok'd Wife* Johann Zoffany (1725-1810)

Oil on canvas

ZOFFANY, who came to England from his native Germany around 1760, was a fine portraitist and principal exponent of the theatrical conversation piece. He was taken up by David Garrick (1717-70), the great actor and manager of the Drury Lane Theatre. Garrick, who was also painted by Hogarth, Reynolds and Gainsborough among others, commissioned Zoffany to paint a series of theatrical conversation pieces featuring him in some of his most famous roles. Here he is seen centre-stage in *The Provok'd Wife,* the Restoration comedy which established the reputation of Sir John Vanbrugh as a dramatist as well as architect (he built Castle Howard in Yorkshire). The painting is a marvellous study in comic exuberance, full of movement and theatrical gesture. Sir John Brute, played by Garrick, has provoked his wife by his churlish treatment of her. While brawling in the street he disguises himself as 'Bonduca Queen of the Welchmen' (although when brought before the magistrate he identifies himself as Lady Brute!) – hence his hilarious appearance in drag.

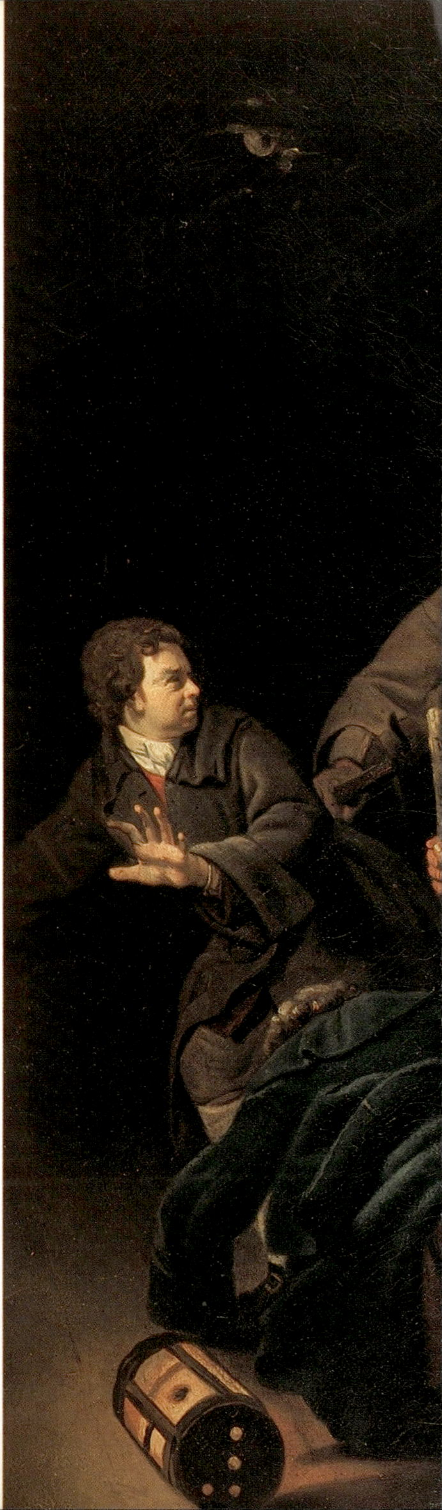

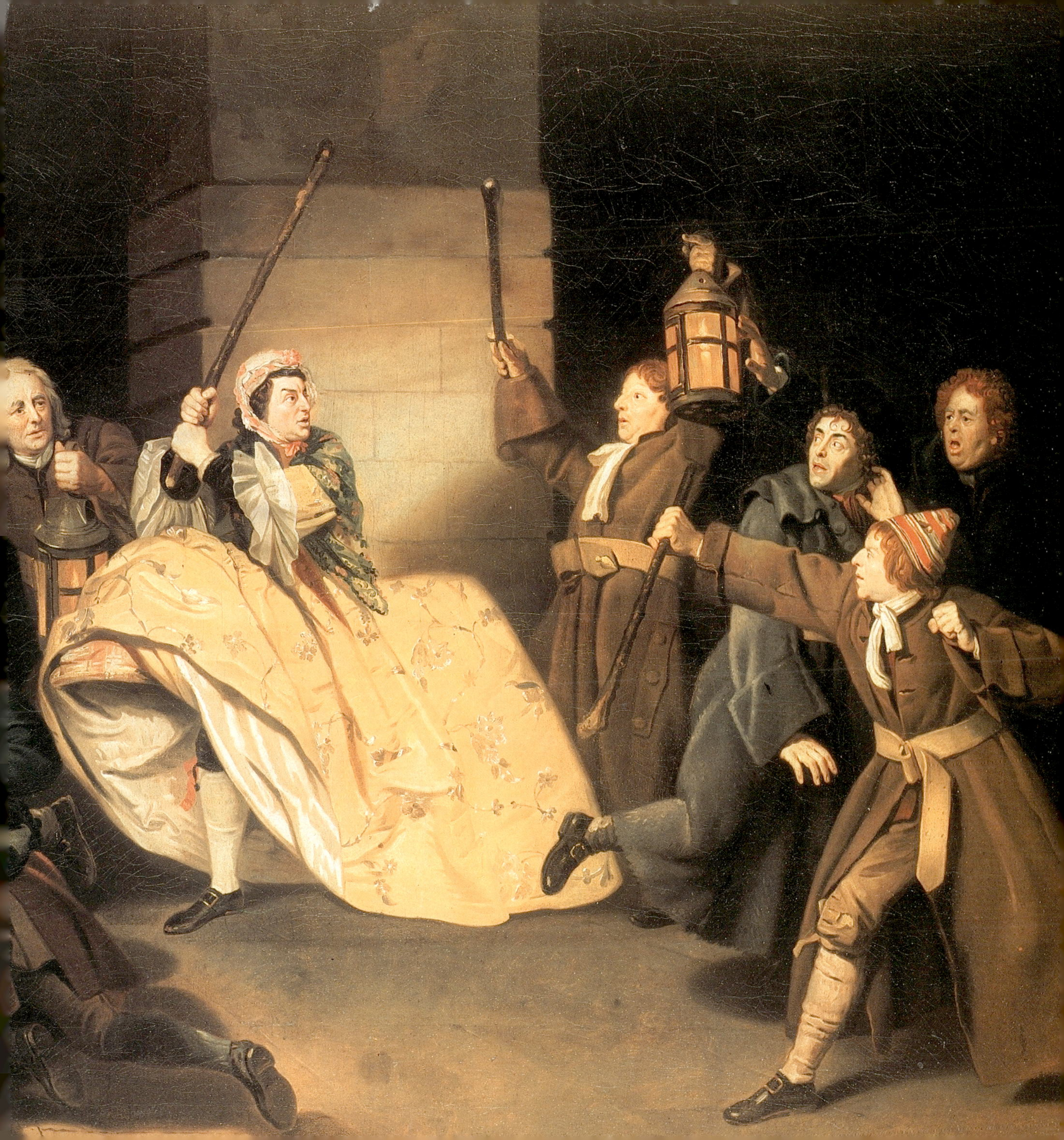

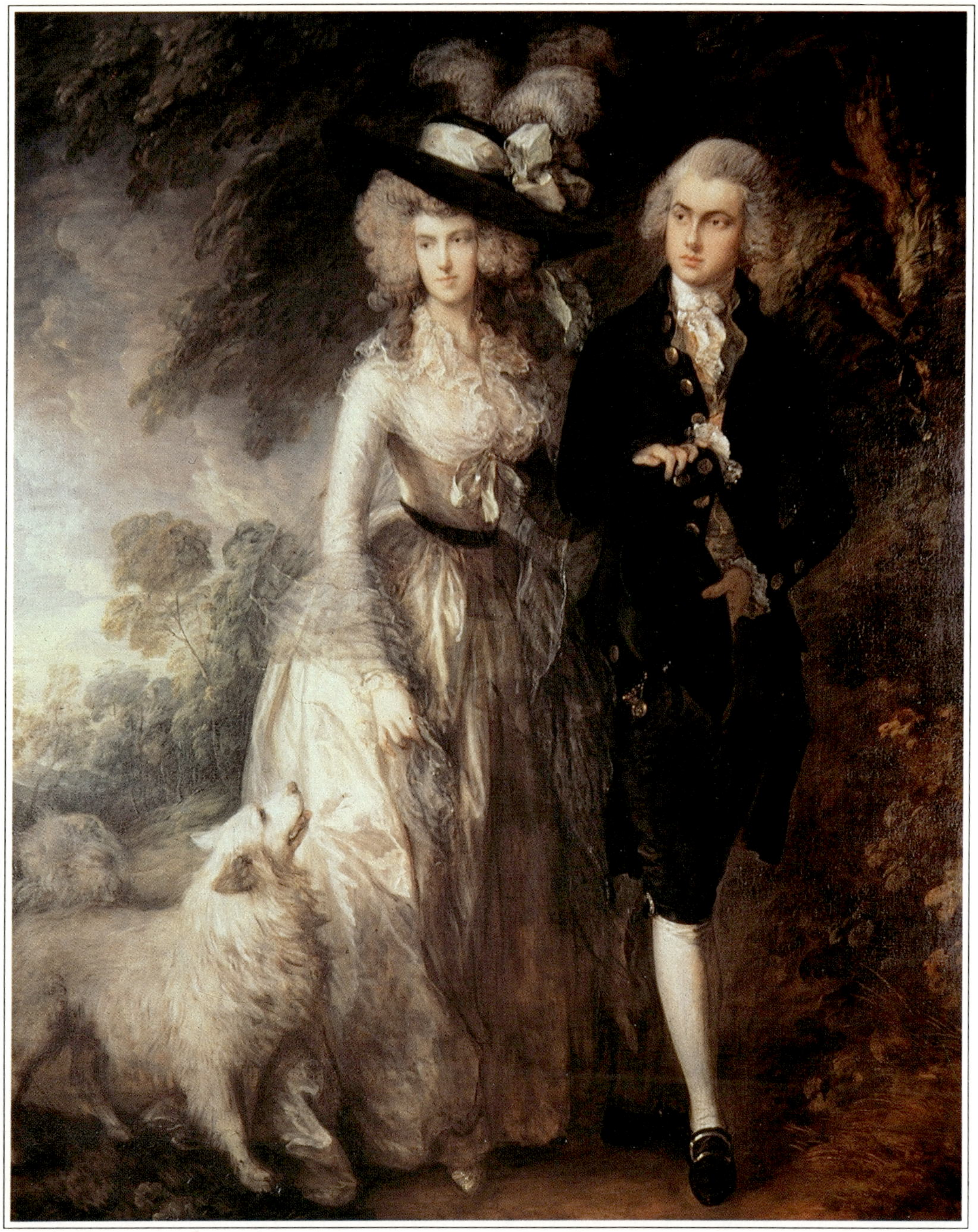

◁ **Mr and Mrs Hallett** Thomas Gainsborough (1727-88)

Oil on canvas

GAINSBOROUGH, a Suffolk man, began his career as a landscape painter, but went on to become perhaps the best-loved English portraitist. He had a special genius for capturing the essence of the English personality, which he does brilliantly in his painting of the newly-wed Mr and Mrs Hallett. This double portrait, also known as *The Morning Walk,* is an example of a new concept of portraiture introduced by Gainsborough. The pose is not static but conveys a sense of movement: the Halletts appear to have paused only momentarily in their stroll down the garden walk – they are not looking out of the picture but to the side, as though some unseen person has temporarily interrupted their tête-à-tête. William Hallett and Elizabeth Stephen were married in July 1785 and this is their nuptial portrait, painted in the autumn following their honeymoon. As well as being an excellent likeness of this handsome, highly fashionable couple, it is also a mood portrait, a sensitive evocation of young romantic love (at the time of their wedding the Halletts were both 21).

▷ **The Duchess of Devonshire and Her Daughter**
Sir Joshua Reynolds (1723-92)

Oil on canvas

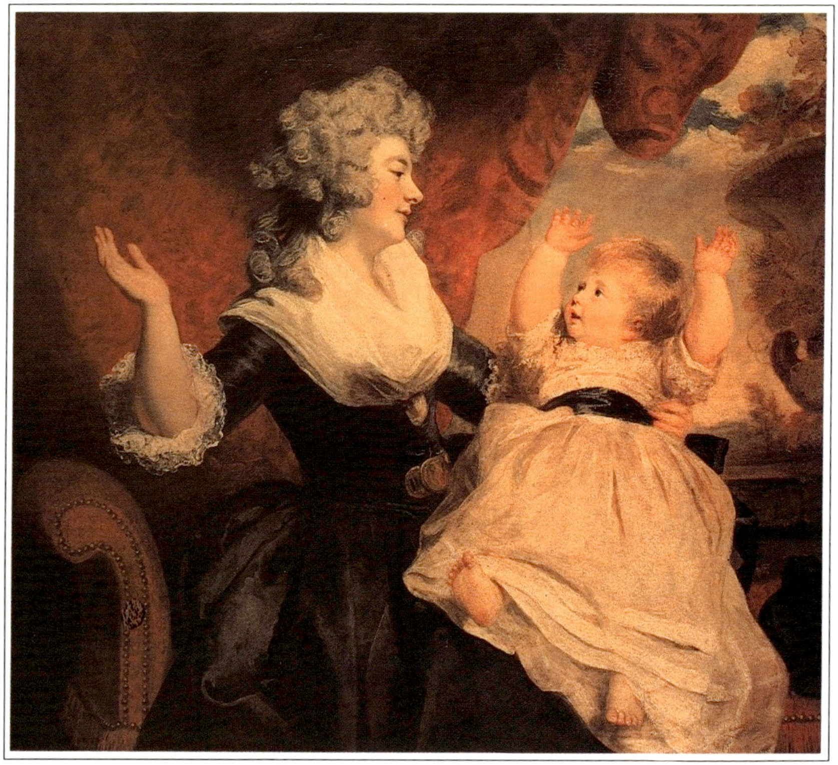

IF GAINSBOROUGH was the best-loved English portraitist, Reynolds, his great rival, was the most eminent: when he died in 1792 the pall-bearers at his funeral consisted of three dukes, two marquesses, three earls, one viscount and one baron. Reynolds began his career as a portraitist in 1743 and in 1768 became the first president of the Royal Academy. Although he favoured the Neo-Classical style, he painted more relaxed and intimate portraits too, and this is one of them: Georgiana Duchess of Devonshire (1757-1806), an ancestor of the present Princess of Wales, and her baby daughter, Georgiana Cavendish (1783-1858), later Countess of Carlisle, form a charming study of maternal love. The Duchess gazes raptly at her child while the baby kicks joyfully with her bare feet; both have their arms outstretched as though playing a game, and are clearly captivated with each other. Despite their noble pedigrees, they could be any mother and child caught at a tender moment. It is interesting to contrast this painting, in the Chatsworth Collection, with a portrait Reynolds painted in 1760/1 of Georgiana, Duchess of Devonshire at the age of 3 with her own mother, Georgiana, Countess Spencer (1737-1814). In the earlier painting, in the Althorp Collection, the pose is less spontaneous: the mother is holding her baby more stiffly and is looking out of the picture, not at the infant.

▷ **Lady Hamilton as a Baccante**
George Romney (1734-1802)

Oil on canvas

ROMNEY, WHO WAS born in Lancashire in 1734, first worked as a portrait painter in Lancaster and Kendal, then went to London in 1762 where he soon built up a busy practice. He fell in love with Emma Hart, as she then was, the daughter of a Cheshire blacksmith, after being introduced to her in 1782 by her lover, Charles Greville. Romney painted Emma many times – 23 portraits of her are recorded. His love was not requited, however – in 1794, after a liaison of 10 years, Emma married Greville's uncle, the diplomat Sir William Hamilton. It was while her husband was ambassador in Naples that Emma met Horatio Nelson after his triumph at the Battle of the Nile in 1798. Romney's portrait of her reflects his taste for the Neo-Classical: he liked to introduce classical allusions, costume and poses into his portraits. Here Emma is portrayed as an attendant of Bacchus, God of Wine.

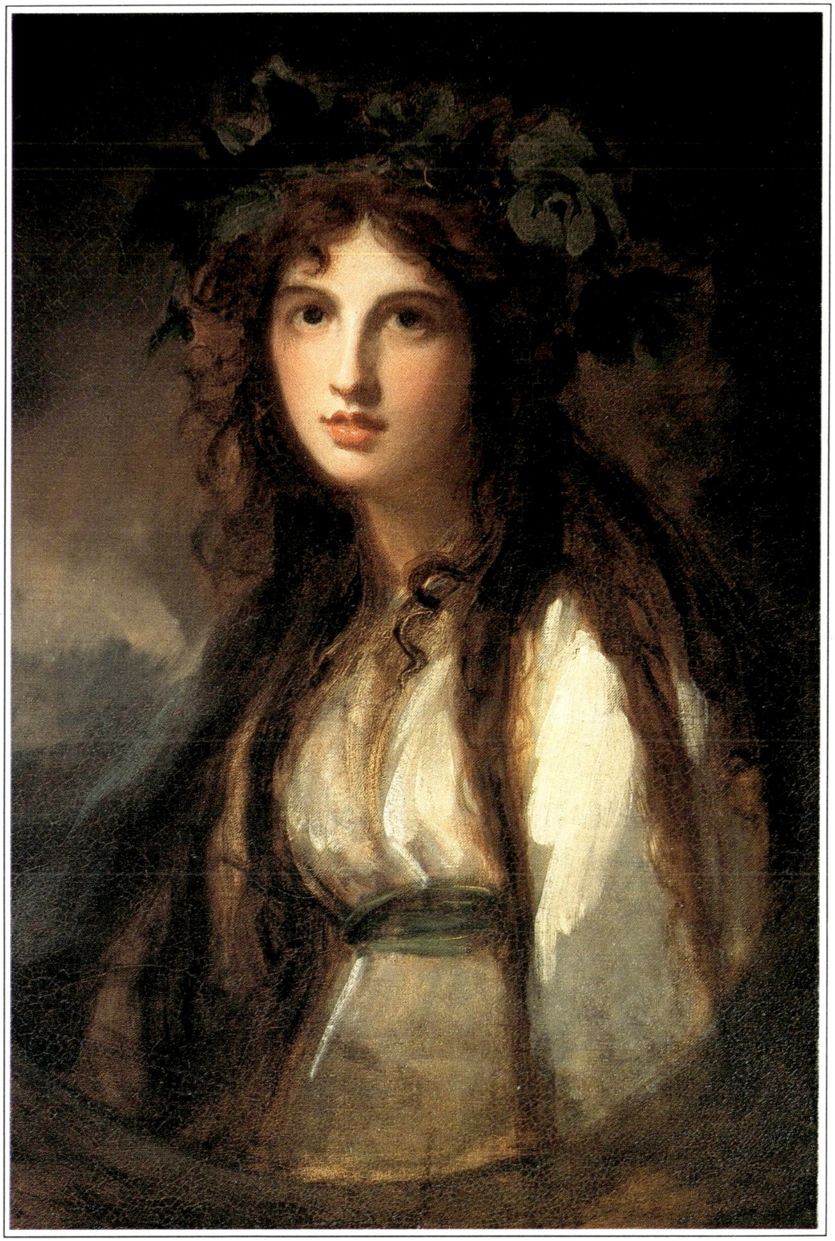

▷ Mr and Mrs Thomas Mifflin
John Singleton Copley (1737-1815)

Oil on canvas

COPLEY, THE FIRST truly great American painter, was born in Boston, Massachusetts. Self-taught, he began painting at 15 and had achieved eminence by 21. His services as a portraitist were much in demand by a relatively unsophisticated but highly prosperous pioneering New England clientele, whose main requirement was a close likeness to be preserved for their heirs and posterity. By 1774 Copley had painted 350 portraits, a clear indication of his success. The poses he used were staid, unfrivolous and fairly limited, like the majority of his sitters, but his sense of realism and perception of character are penetrating, as can be seen in this double portrait of the Mifflins, prominent Philadelphians on a visit to Boston. Thomas Mifflin, a radical Whig, later became governor of Pennsylvania. Here he gazes proudly and proprietorially at his wife, who is shown in an industrious pose, working at a fringe loom. They are clearly a couple who have every reason to be pleased with themselves. The spider-leg table in the picture is characteristic of Copley's interest in furniture, which he liked to introduce into his portraits – Boston was renowned for its cabinet-makers. This portrait was painted in 1773, the year of the Boston Tea Party: two years later Copley sailed for England, where his work had impressed Reynolds and others, and settled permanently in London.

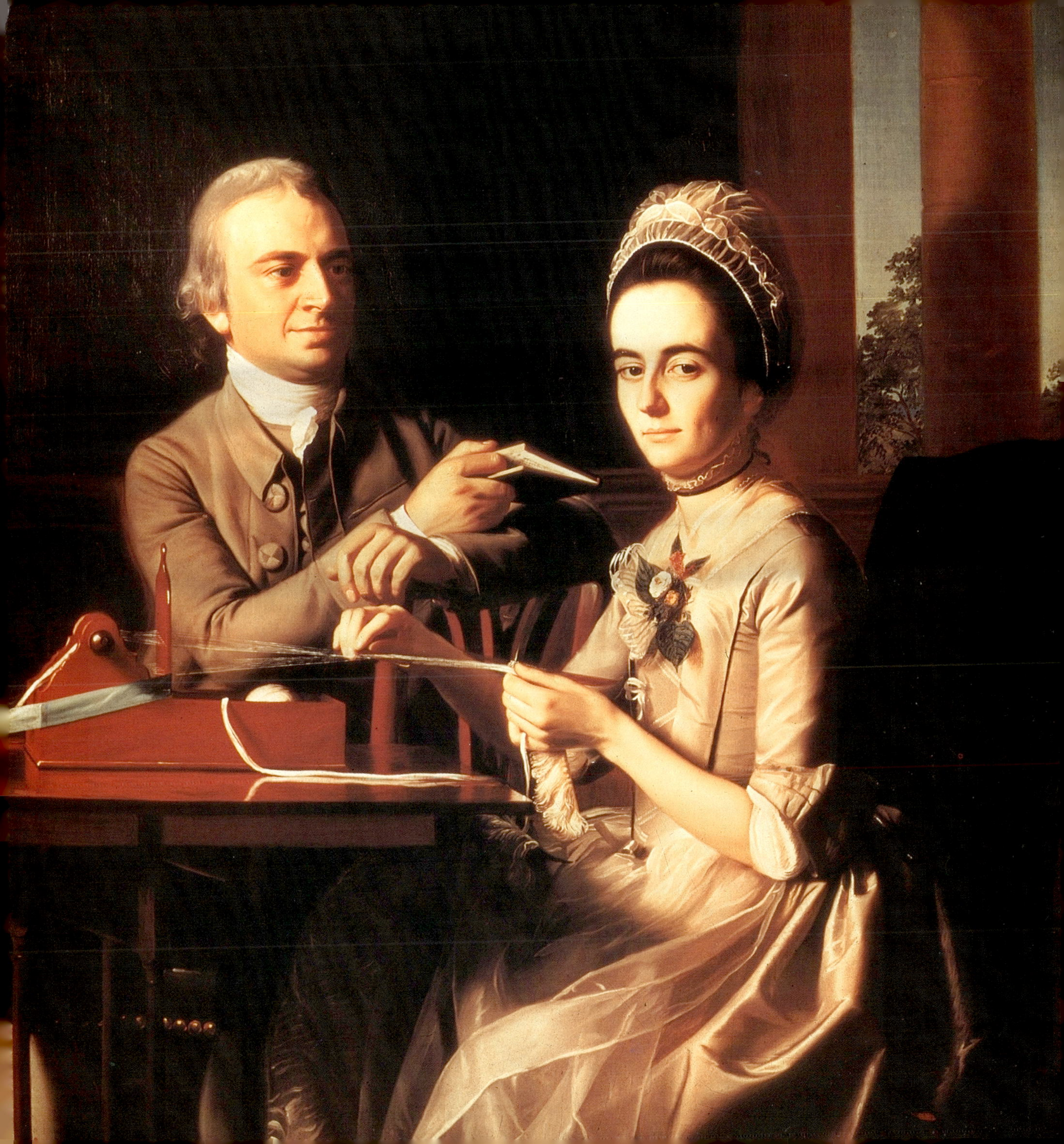

▷ Anna von Escher von Muralt
Angelica Kauffmann (1741-1807)

Oil on canvas

ANGELICA KAUFFMANN, the only woman portraitist represented in this book, was herself the daughter of a painter. She was born in Switzerland in 1741 but lived in Italy during her childhood. She helped her father with decorative work from an early age and was something of a child prodigy, for she painted a portrait of the Bishop of Como at the age of only 12. She went to Rome in 1763 and in 1765 was taken up by the wife of the British ambassador. Angelica was both beautiful and talented as a musician as well as artist, and when she arrived in England in 1766 she enjoyed a tremendous personal and professional success. She was much admired by Reynolds, who did a lot to help her; he painted her portrait in 1769 and their names have been linked romantically. Angelica was a founder member of the Royal Academy and exhibited in every RA show from 1769 to 1782. She did decorative work for the Adam brothers and married the decorative artist Antonio Zucchi in 1781. Angelica Kauffman was at her best painting female sitters, as in this portrait, which also displays her pronounced taste for Neo-Classicism, in which she was influenced by Reynolds. The pose, the gauzy drapery of the costume and the cypress tree and classical temple in the background are all familiar Neo-Classical devices.

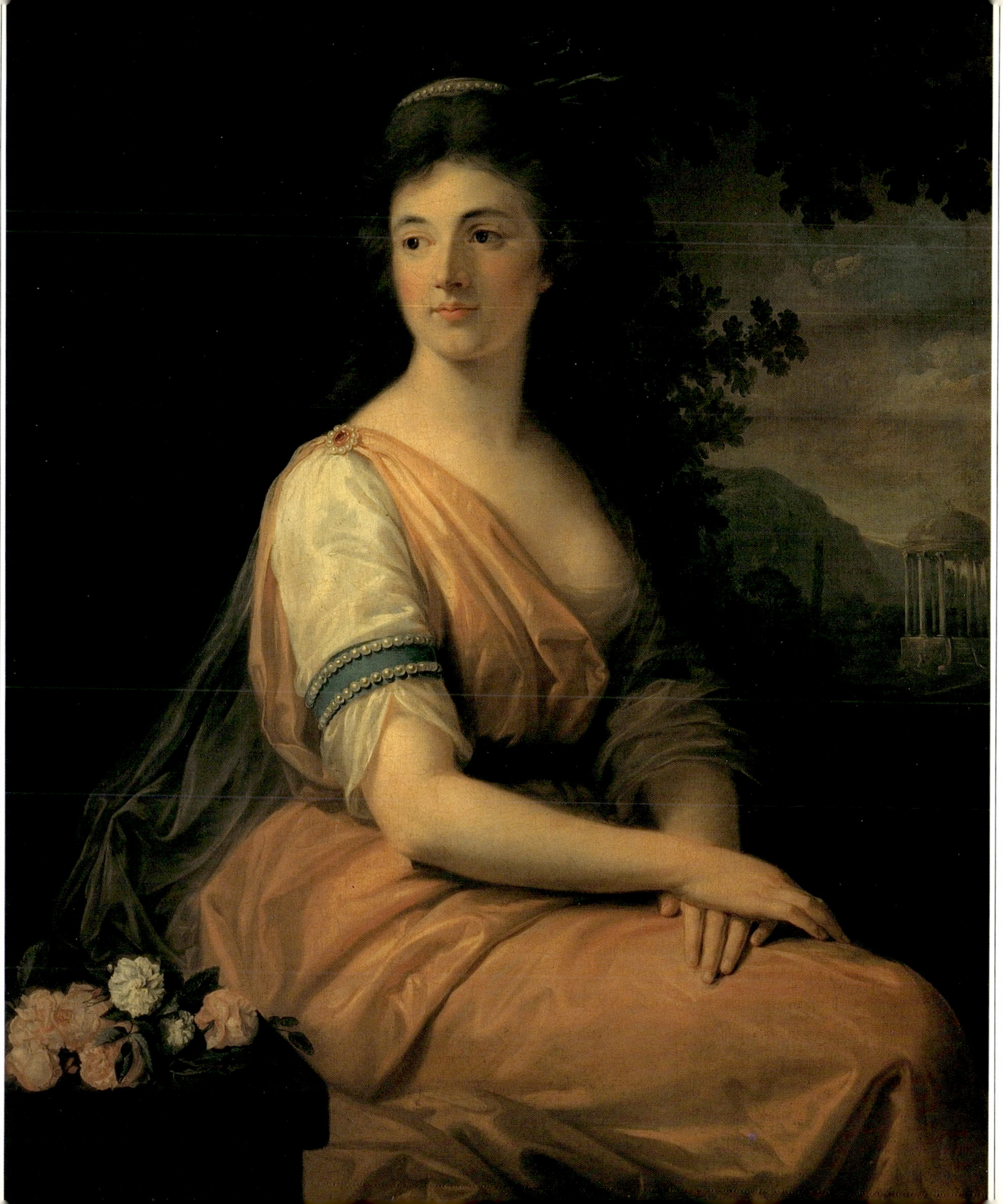

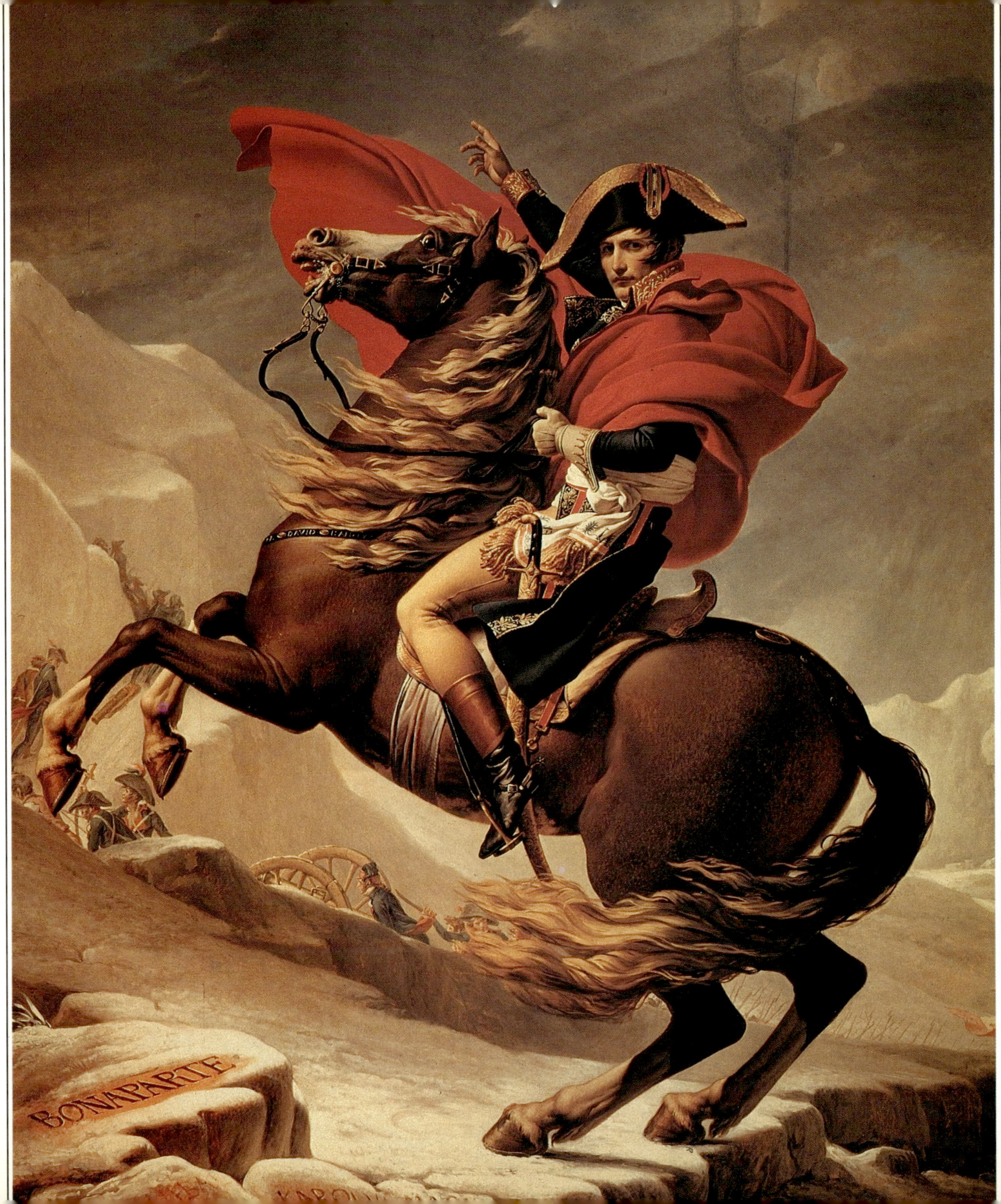
BONAPARTE

◁ **Napoleon Crossing the Alps** Jacques Louis David (1748-1825)

Oil on canvas

DAVID, WHO WAS BORN in Paris in 1748, was artistic director of the Revolutionary regime for four years, organizing festivals and pageants for propaganda purposes. He later became an ardent Bonapartist. Napoleon made David Government Painter in 1800 and asked him to paint a romantic equestrian portrait of him following his victory at the battle of Marengo in June. 'I want to be painted calm, on a fiery horse,' he said, adding that he was less concerned with a realistic likeness than that 'genius should be there' – although he stipulated that his own horse should be depicted to the life. David met the request perfectly in his heroic portrait which shows Napoleon impassive and totally in command of both his rearing steed and the situation, dwarfing the tiny figures of the soldiers below. His uniform, which David obtained from his valet, was the very one he wore at Marengo. He is shown crossing the St Bernard Pass, although ironically he actually made the crossing on a mule.

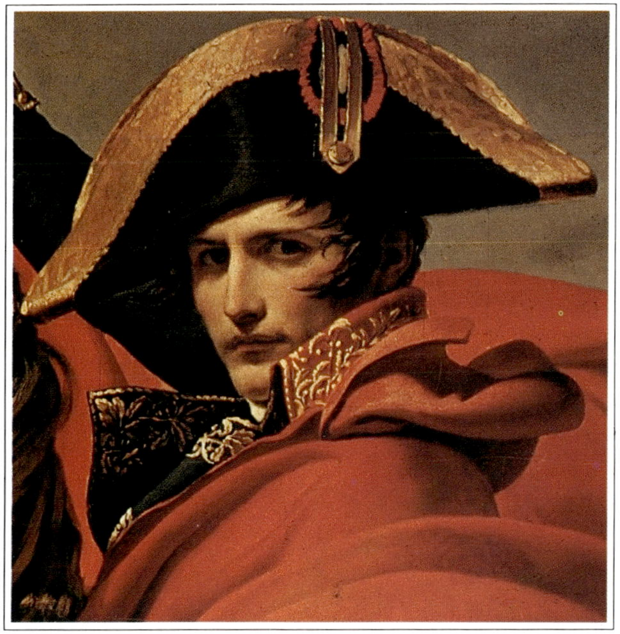

Detail

On the rocks bottom left are inscribed the names of Hannibal and Charlemagne, Napoleon's illustrious predecessors to cross the mighty Alps. The drama and excitement of this terrific portrait are enhanced by the perilously rugged landscape and ominously stormy sky.

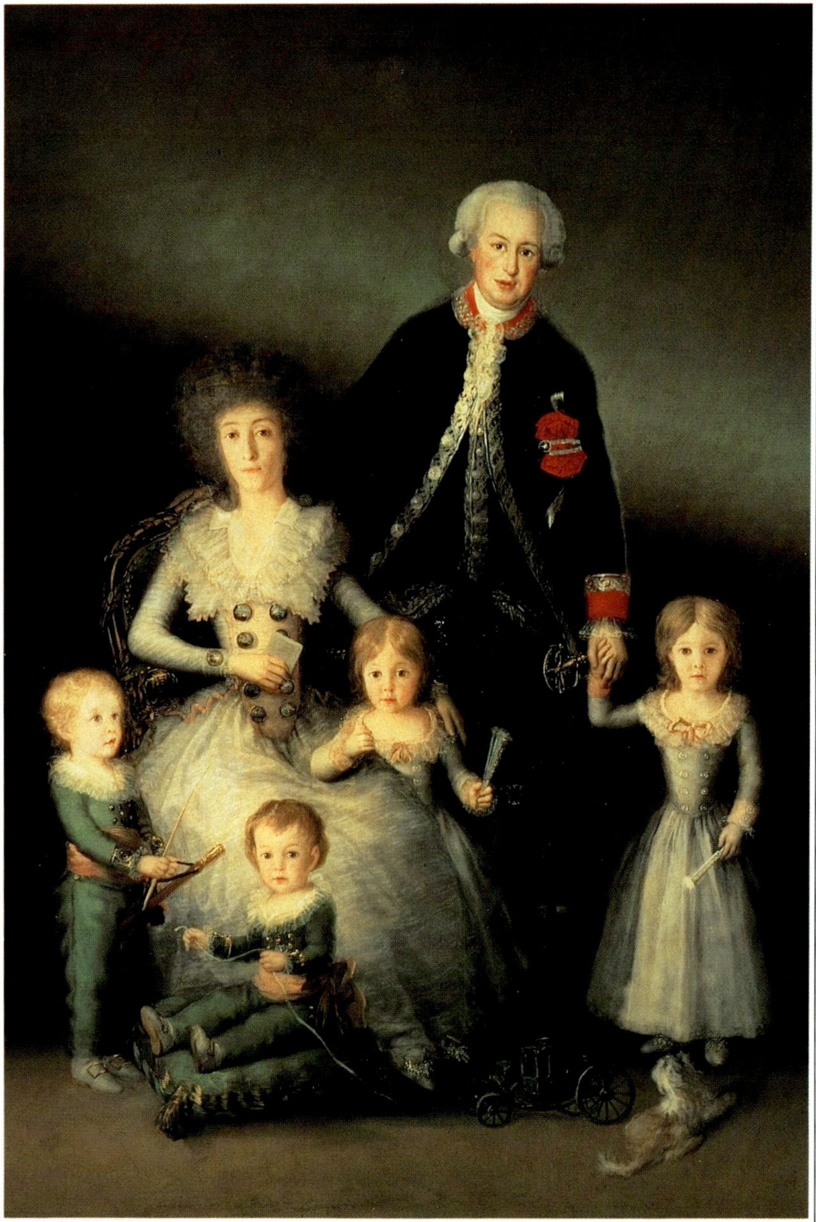

◁ **The Duke of Osuna and His Family** Francisco Goya (1746-1828)

Oil on canvas

BORN NEAR SARAGOSSA in 1746, Goya became a successor of Velazquez as official painter to the Spanish royal court, and he stands at the crossroads between the Old Master and modern styles of portraiture. His portraits are brilliant in their stark simplicity, subtly varied richness of tone and profound analysis of character. This family group, painted in 1788, is full of interest. For a start, this is clearly a young family – the features of the Duke and Duchess are remarkably youthful beneath their elaborate wigs. The portrayal of their children illustrates Goya's special skill in child portraiture. He has included many details which indicate his sympathy with children. Both sisters carry fans and wear dresses like their mother's, like little adults, but one holds her father's hand while the other leans on her mother's knee. Their brothers are portrayed with their toys – a carriage on a string and a bow and arrow.

▷ **Mary Wright Alsop**
Ralph Earl (1751-1801)

Oil on canvas

EARL, BORN IN 1751 in Massachusetts, excelled, like Copley (see page 44), at portraying the descendants of America's Founding Fathers. This portrait is of particular interest, being one of a pair, mother and daughter. Mary Wright Alsop was the only child and sole heir of Joseph and Hannah Wright; her father was instrumental in developing Middleton, Connecticut, as a thriving port and made a fortune as a result. Mary married his business partner, Richard Alsop, at the age of 20. Both families were Episcopalians. When Mary was widowed in 1776, a year after her father's death, she was left with eight children, all of whom went on to be successful, and an enormous estate and international mercantile business to run. The portraits of these two formidable widows were commissioned in 1792. Earl's painting brings out all the intelligence, resourcefulness and strength of character of this remarkable woman, pictured in her parental home.

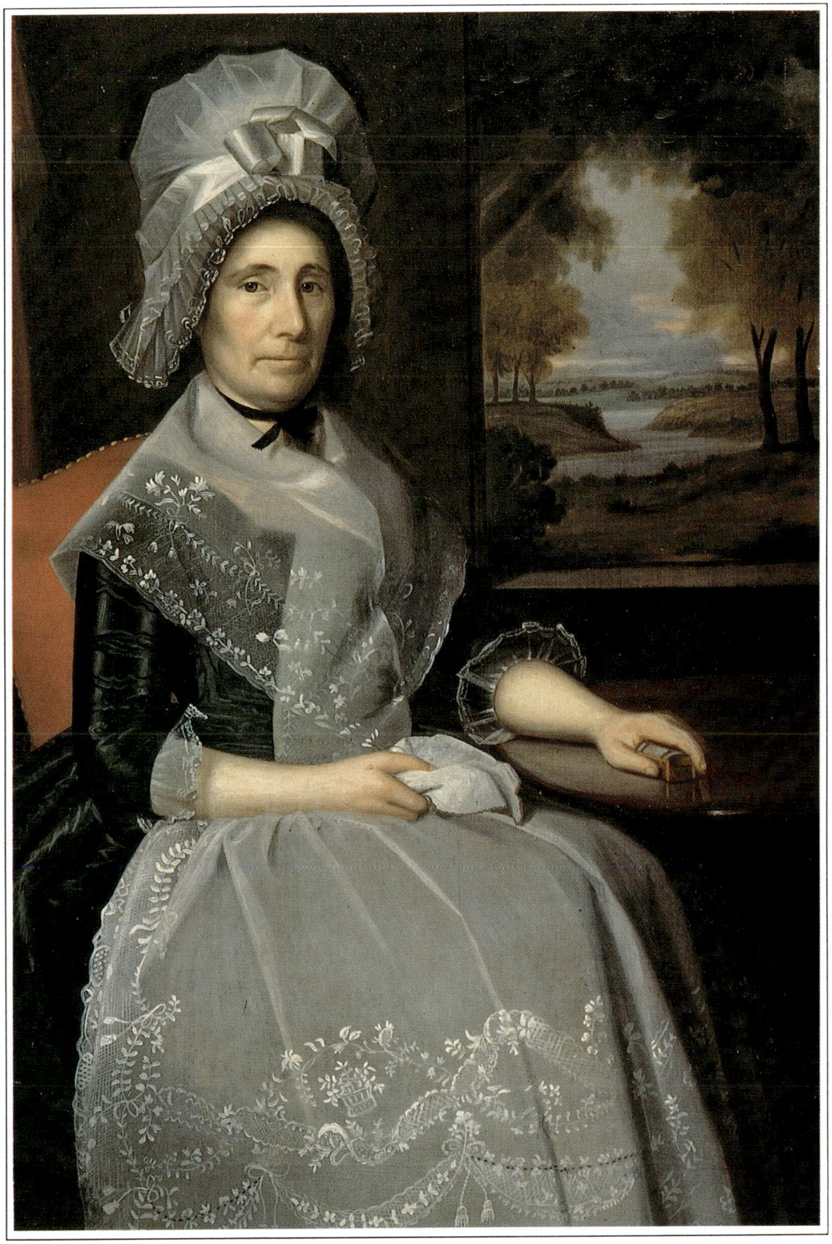

▷ **Madame Moitessier** Jean-Auguste Ingres (1780-1867)

Oil on canvas

INGRES, BORN NEAR PARIS in 1780, was the son of a painter and ornamental sculptor, and a pupil of David. He was commissioned to paint Madame Inès Moitessier in 1844. The plan had originally been to include her small daughter Catherine, but Ingres found the child unbearable, and the idea was abandoned. Seven years later the portrait had still not been painted, and after receiving a polite reminder from his client, Ingres painted a portrait of Madame Moitessier standing, wearing an off-shoulder black dress with pink roses in her hair. In 1856, five years later, the seated portrait was finished. Classical antiquity was always a source of inspiration for Ingres, and the pose here was derived from a personification of Arcadia in a Roman fresco from Herculaneum. It suits the Junoesque presence of Madame Moitessier perfectly, and the use of the mirror reflection cleverly shows off her classical profile and magnificent shoulders. All the luxury and opulence of the Second Empire are evident in the richness of the rose-printed silk dress, the handsome amethyst bracelet and the sumptuous setting of Madame Moitessier's fashionable drawing-room.

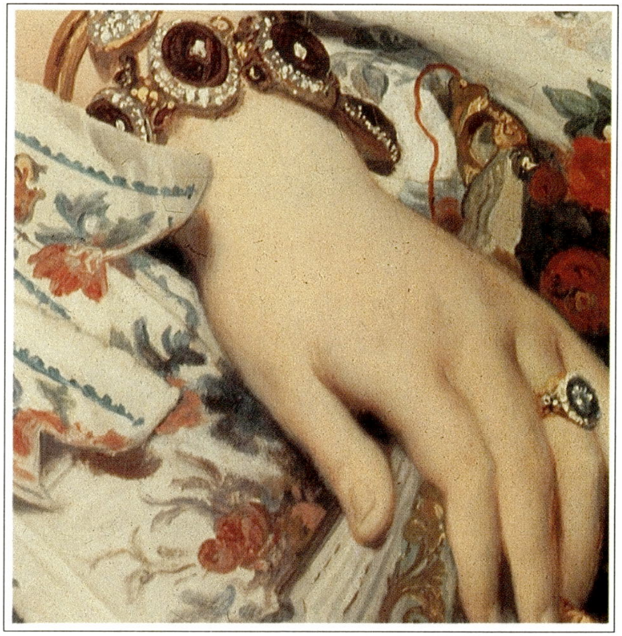

Detail

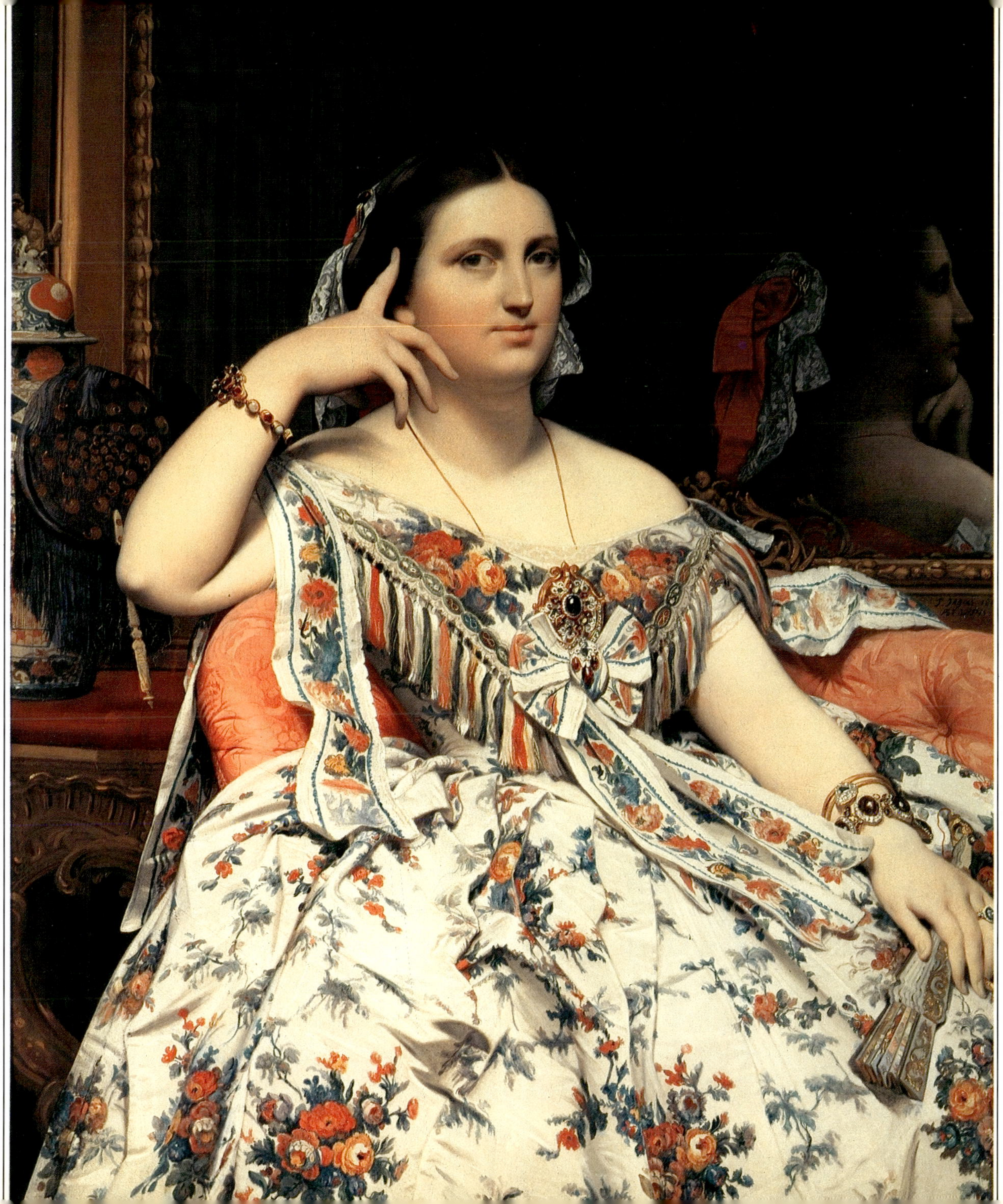

▷ **A Woman Knitting** Jean-François Millet (1814-75)

Oil on canvas

MILLET HAD A LIFELONG fascination with the peasant life of his native Normandy (he was born near Gréville in 1814). Himself the son of a peasant (though his father was a gifted organist and calligrapher, and Millet received a good education), he retained a close relationship with the land, which he knew intimately in all its moods and seasons. Rural depopulation as a result of emigration to towns was a cause of national concern in France in Millet's time, giving his painting special resonance and importance. Millet expressed endless pastoral themes and activities in his work – sowing, harvesting, gleaning, sheep-shearing, grafting, apple-picking, hoeing, baking bread, carding wool, bird-nesting, potato-planting, and so on. He painted this portrait of an anonymous countrywoman knitting in 1860. Her absorption in her task seems to indicate that even while resting from her labours in the field she did not like to remain idle.

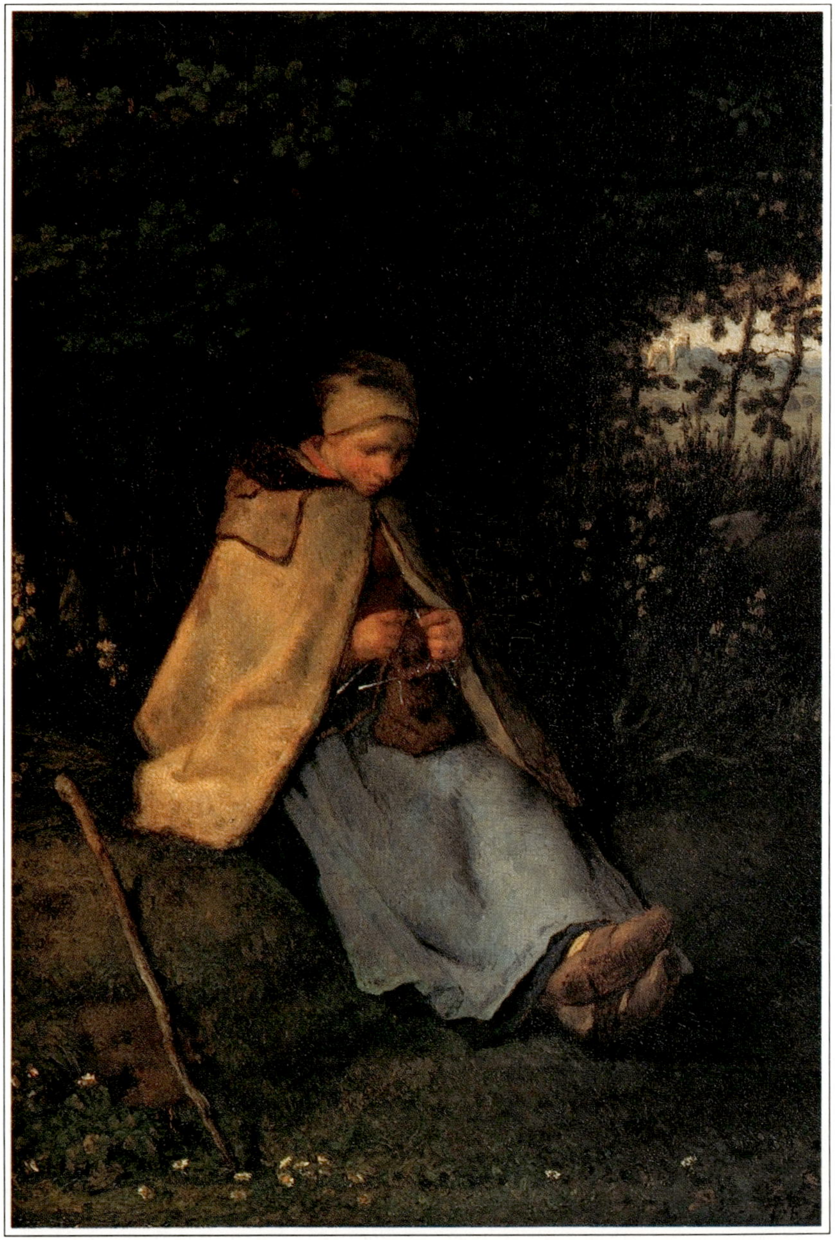

▷ **The Princes in the Tower**
Sir John Everett Millais (1829-96)

Oil on canvas

MILLAIS WAS A CHILD prodigy, entering the Royal Academy Schools at the age of only 10, having already received a silver medal from the Royal Society of Arts. Eight years later, with fellow students Gabriel Rossetti and Holman Hunt, he founded the Pre-Raphaelite Brotherhood, named from the trio's admiration for the early Italian painters before Raphael. Millais, who had a brilliant career as a highly fashionable society portrait painter, was also famous for his historical costume portraits. *The Princes in the Tower* shows Millais's considerable skill as a portraitist of children, and conveys all the intense emotional impact characteristic of the Pre-Raphaelites. It is a picture of isolation and apprehension: the children, wrongfully imprisoned and later cruelly murdered by their usurper uncle, Richard III, hold each other by the hand, the younger boy clutching his elder brother for reassurance.

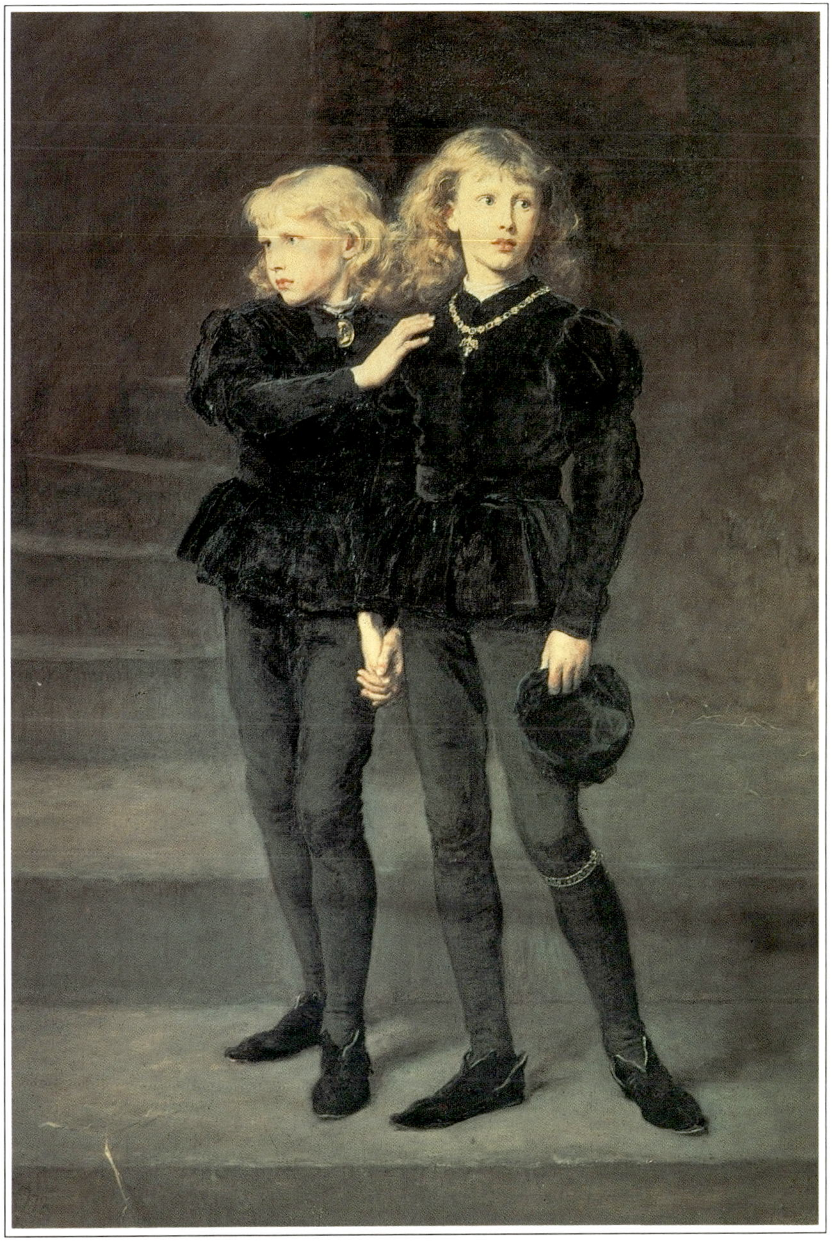

▷ **Monet Painting in his Studio Boat**
Edouard Manet (1832-83)

Oil on canvas

HIGHLY CONTROVERSIAL in his own time for his innovative techniques, Manet was a true precursor of modern art. He was a hero of Impressionism, which he inspired by his rebellious example, but never regarded himself as one of the Impressionists, although he experimented with their techniques. One of these was the creation of the shimmering effect of light on water, which Manet employs to superb effect in this portrait of his friend, the Impressionist Claude Monet, painting in his studio boat. Monet built this floating studio to enable himself to work as close as possible to the water, the element that intrigued him most. Manet painted this picture in the summer of 1874, when he was at his family home at Gennevilliers, on the opposite bank of the Seine to Argenteuil (now an industrial suburb, then a riverside country retreat). 1874 was the year of the disastrous first Impressionist Exhibition in Paris. Manet did not contribute to the exhibition, but helped Monet out financially by paying the rent on his house at Argenteuil. His painting of Monet at work was a kind of homage to his friend's achievements. Madame Camille Monet, the artist's wife, whom Manet also painted in Monet's garden at Argenteuil, is seated by the entrance to the cabin.

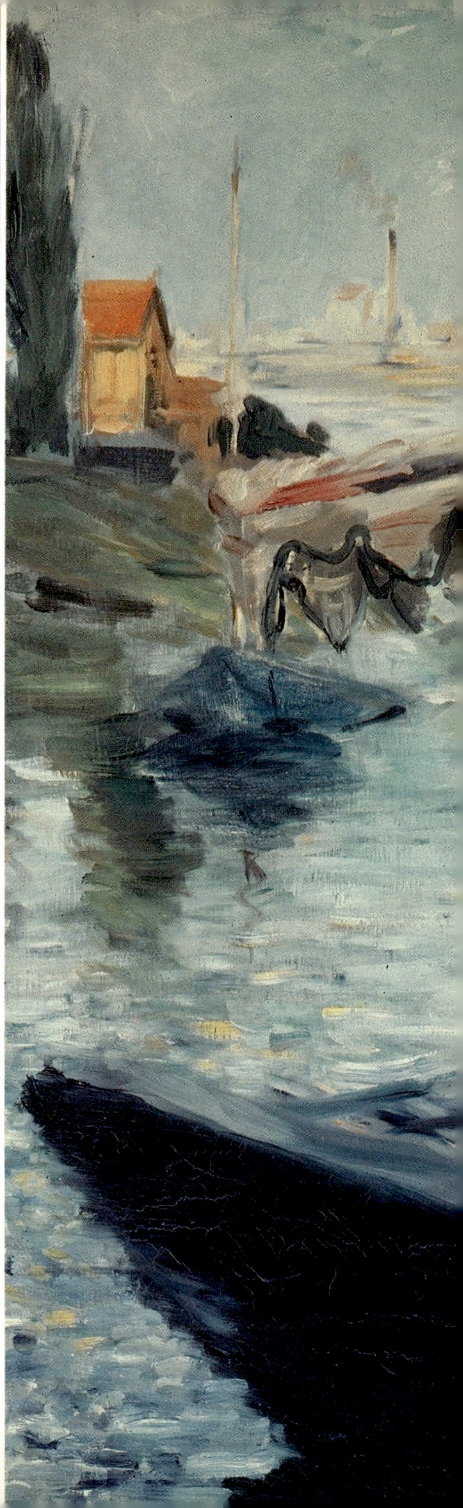

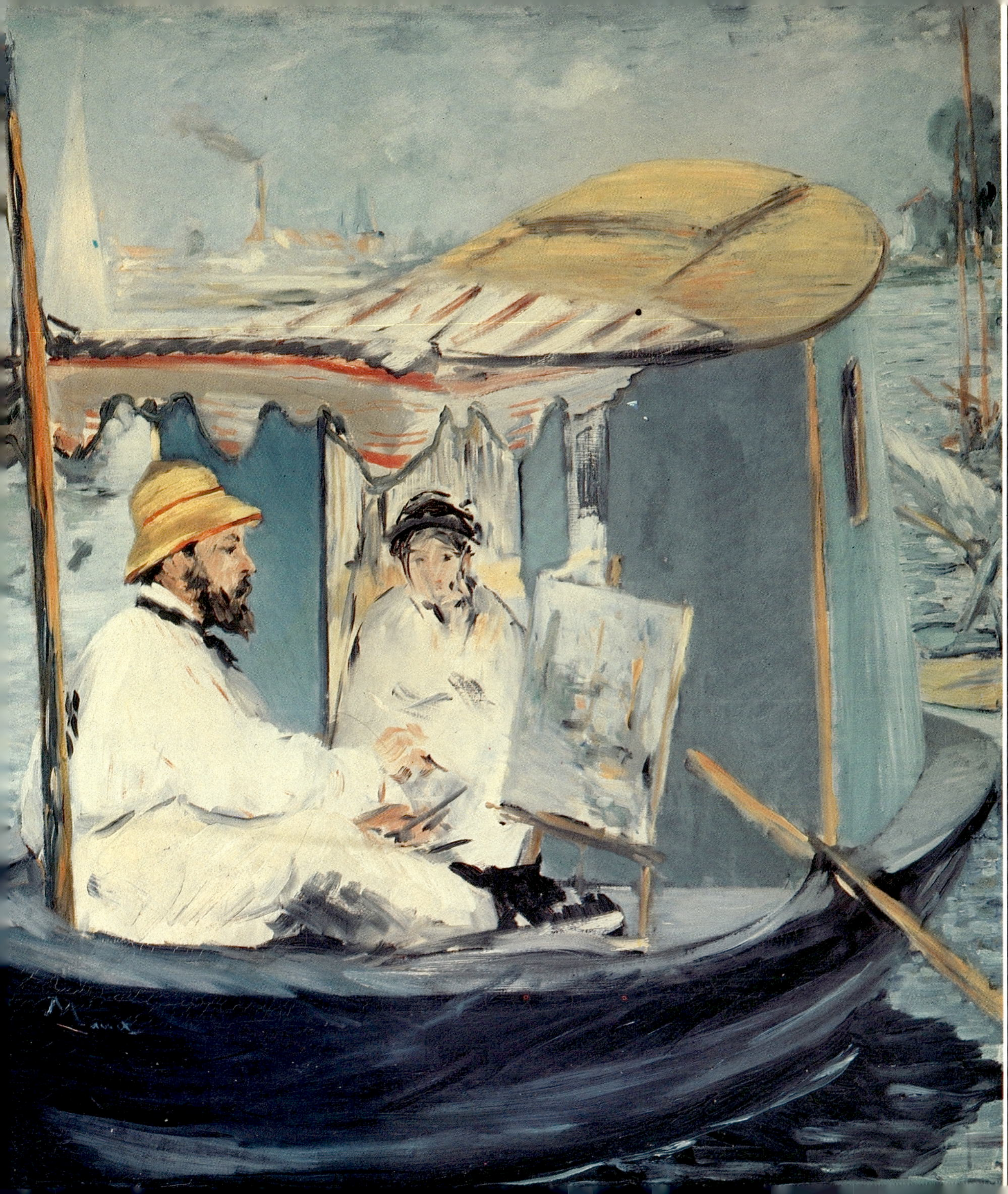

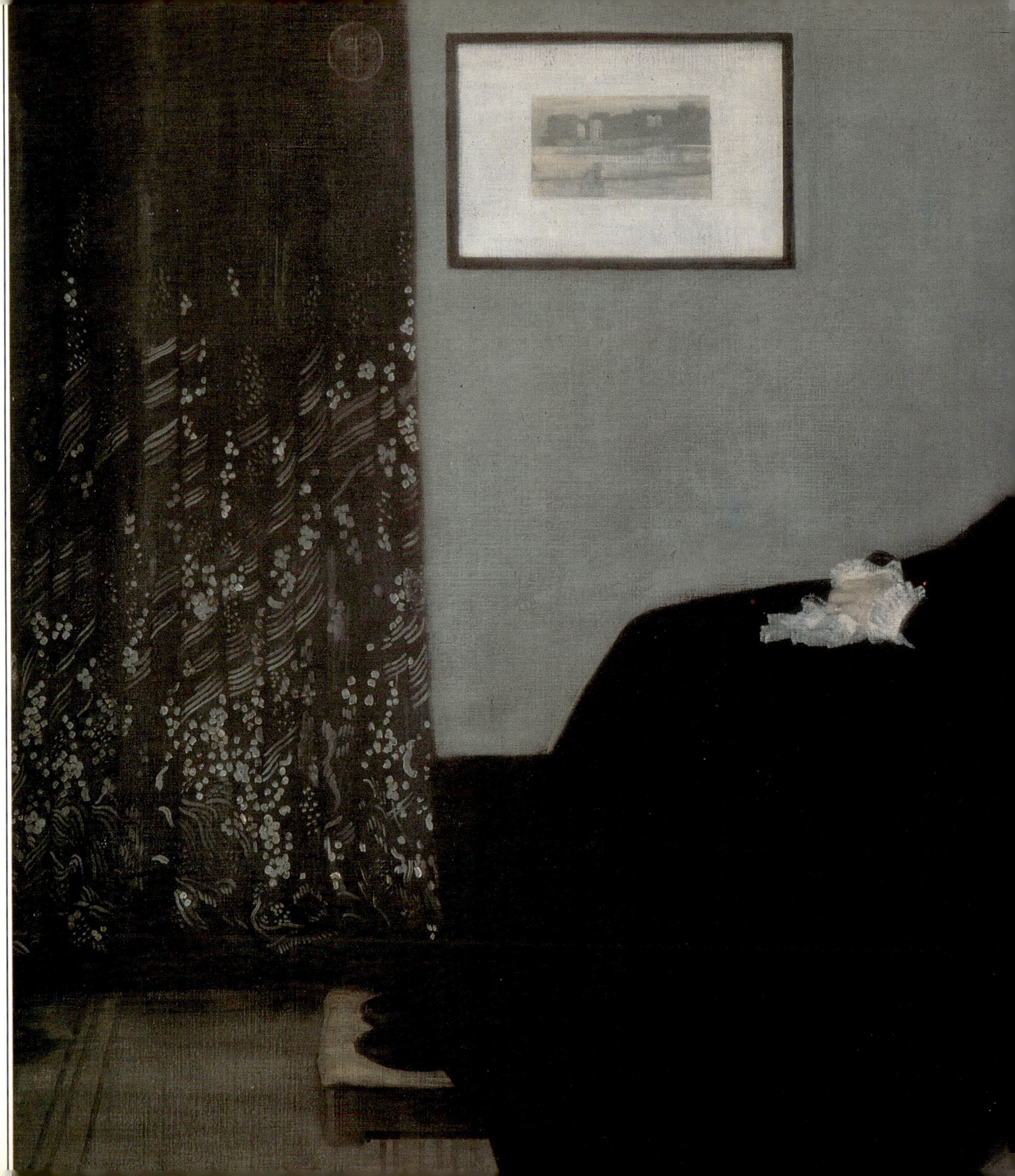

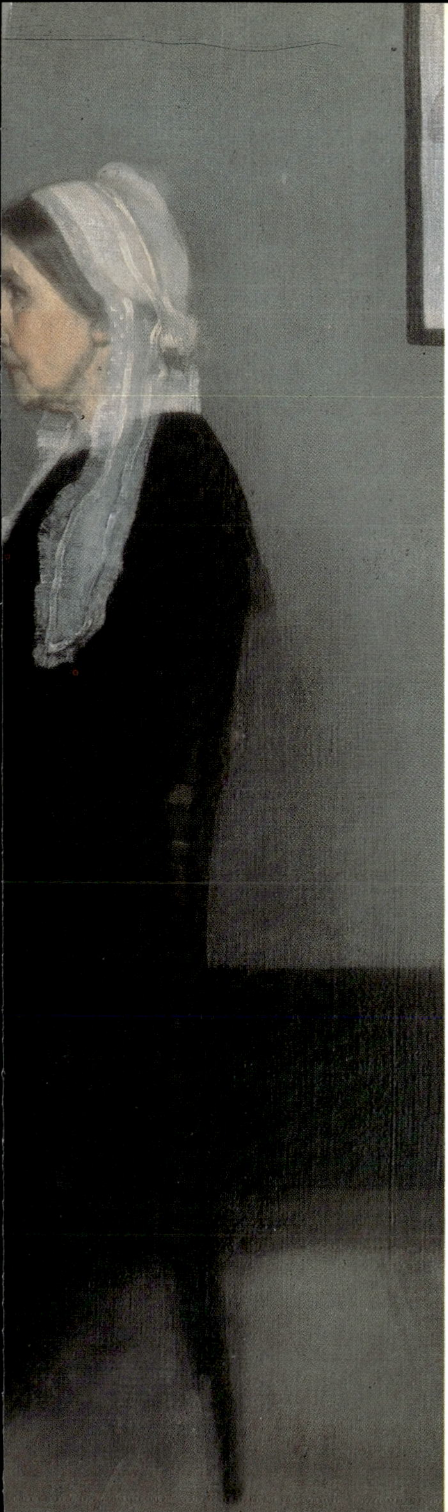

◁ **Portrait of the Artist's Mother**
James McNeill Whistler (1834-1903)

Oil on canvas

BORN IN MASSACHUSETTS, Whistler spent most of his working life in London and Paris, where he enjoyed a reputation as aesthete, wit and eccentric in bohemian circles. He conducted a series of experiments with colour and its application which he described as Arrangements, Caprices, Symphonies, Harmonies and Nocturnes – musical terms denoting the synthesis of the arts, an idea Whistler took from the Symbolist poets. This portrait of his mother, one of Whistler's earliest, was titled *Arrangement in Black and Gray.* It was first exhibited at the Royal Academy in 1872. Whistler chose a profile pose in this very sober yet intense painting. Austere and restrained as the colour tones and figure are, the mood is one of repose rather than severity. With her tranquil expression beneath her old-fashioned bonnet, her hands clasped in her lap and her feet placed neatly side by side, Mrs Whistler seems totally at peace with herself and her surroundings – a picture of serenity in old age. The background against which she is silhouetted is almost blank except for the depiction of one of Whistler's own etchings, Black Lion Wharf, which formed part of a series he did of the River Thames. In this way all the viewer's attention is focused on the figure of the sitter.

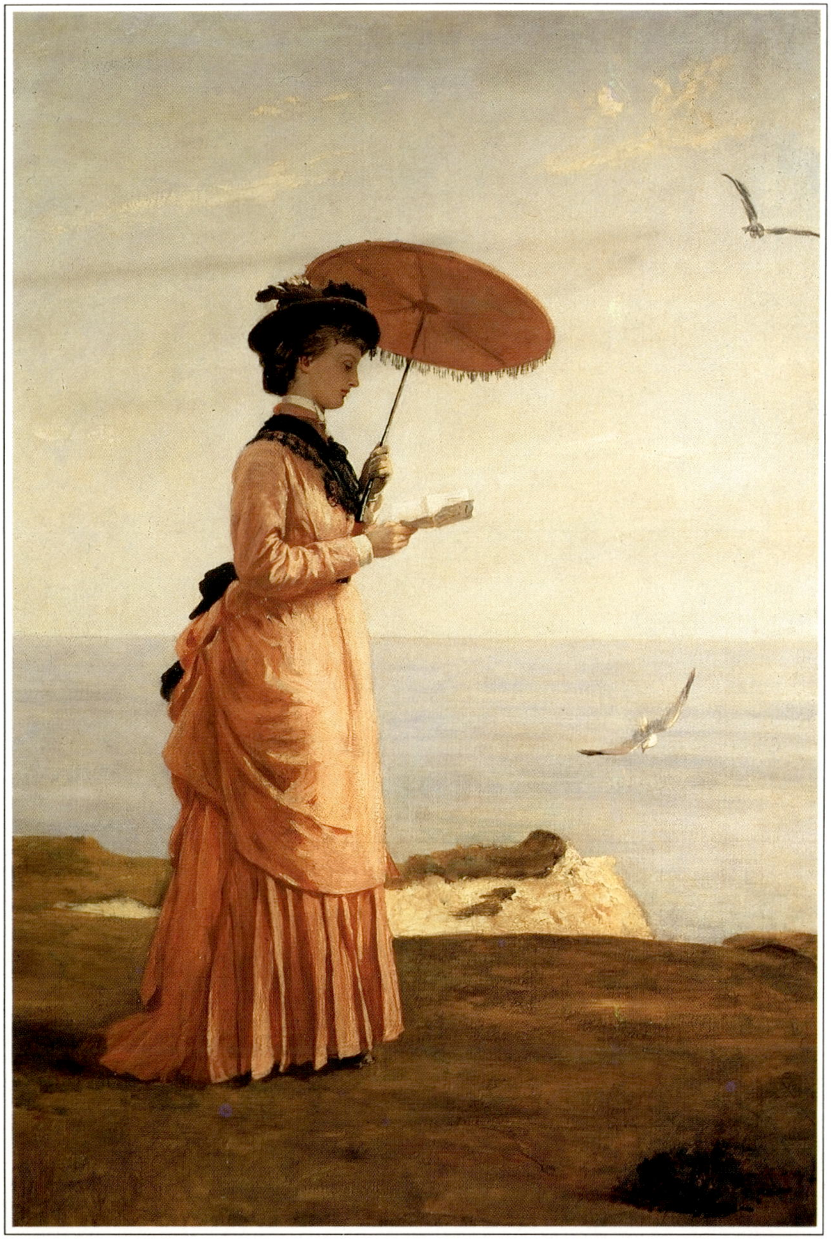

◁ **Lady Tennyson on Afton Downs, Freshwater Bay, Isle of Wight** Valentine Prinsep (1838-1904)

Oil on canvas

VAL PRINSEP was one of the lesser-known artists associated with the Pre-Raphaelite movement. He was commissioned to paint Emily Tennyson (née Sellwood), the wife of the Poet Laureate, on the cliffs close to the Tennysons' beloved home, Farringford, near Freshwater, on the Isle of Wight. Tennyson originally leased the house in 1853, then purchased it 2 years later. The Tennysons spent most of each year in this inspiring and invigorating spot, 'close to the ridge of the noble down', in Tennyson's own words. This is a portrait in which the setting is of particular importance: the wheeling seagulls and the impression of bright sunlight necessitating the use of the protective parasol create a vivid sense of place. Lady Tennyson, who was the sister-in-law of Tennyson's brother Charles, died at the age of 83 in 1896 and is buried in Freshwater churchyard.

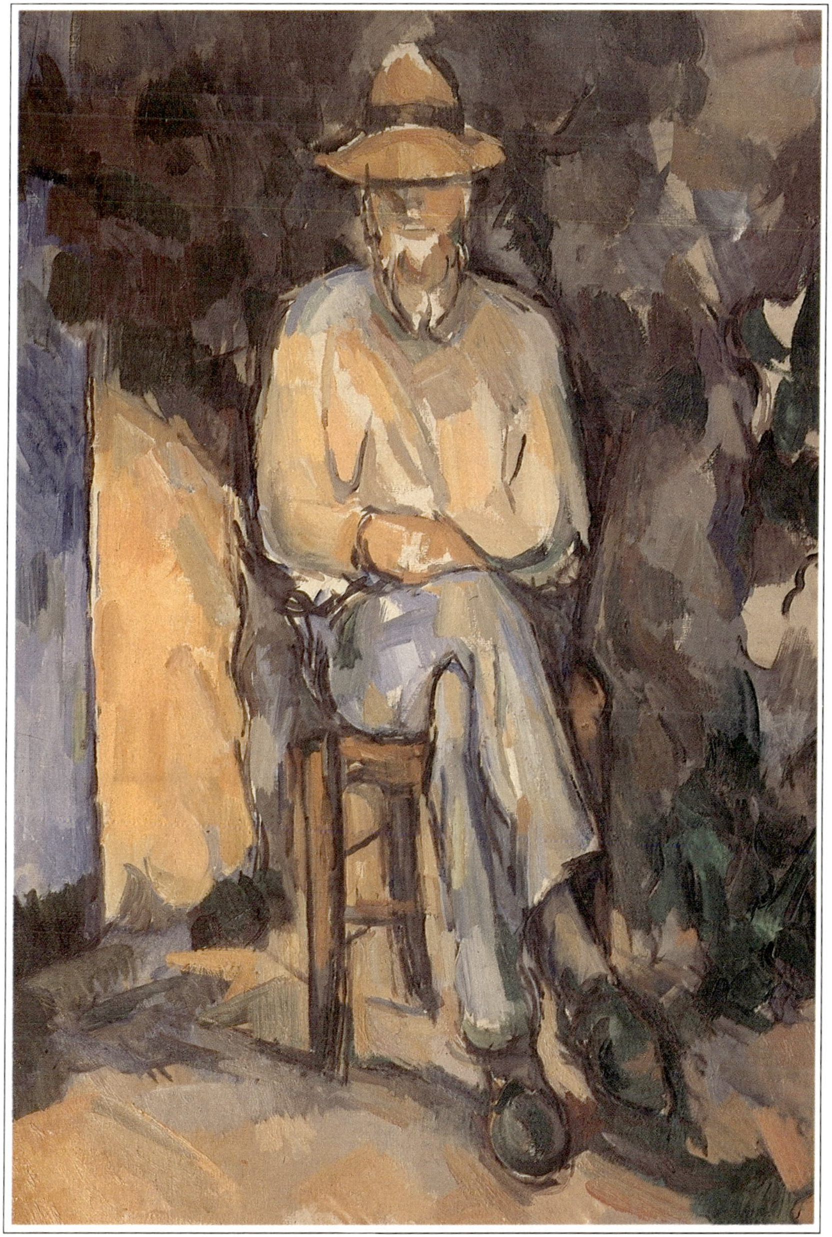

◁ **The Gardener**
Paul Cézanne (1839-1906)

Oil on canvas

CÉZANNE IS WIDELY regarded as the most innovative artist of the 19th century. In his portraits, still-lifes and landscapes, he broke new ground in terms of composition and use of colour. He was a precursor of Cubism, and a tendency to abstraction resulted in his being misunderstood in his own time. Cézanne loved his native Provence, but in 1899 the Jas de Bouffon, the property left to him by his father, and the setting for many of his landscapes, had to be sold. Three years later he had a new studio built on a hill above Aix, in the Chemin des Lauves. It was here, shortly before he died, that he painted this famous portrait of Vallier, his gardener and odd-job man. It is a remarkable evocation of one elderly man by another: one senses a profound understanding between the artist and his subject. Cézanne has painted Vallier with great respect, creating an image of inner strength, self-sufficiency and true nobility.

▷ **Blanche Monet Painting** Claude Monet (1840-1926)

Oil on canvas

CLAUDE MONET was the leader, and is generally regarded as the greatest, of the group of artists known as the Impressionists. In fact it was from one of Monet's paintings *(Impression, Sunrise)* of 1872, depicting the play of light on water, one of the artist's favourite themes, that the term Impressionism was derived. Monet, a highly prolific painter, excelled in both landscapes and portraits, and enjoyed painting members of his family and friends. This portrait of Blanche, the daughter of Monet's second wife, Alice (his first wife, Camille, died tragically in 1879 at the age of 32) combines all these characteristics of his work. The picture is particularly interesting for showing painting within a painting; Blanche's professional working pose, the way she holds her palette and brush while intent on her easel, contrasts with that of her companion, relaxing under a tree with her book. The vivid emerald green of the grass and the sunlit pink and white froth of the blossom in the orchard are typical of Monet's brilliant use of colour to evoke a mood. So are the brush-strokes, by means of which the paint is applied in a myriad small dabs, conveying an impression of flickering light.

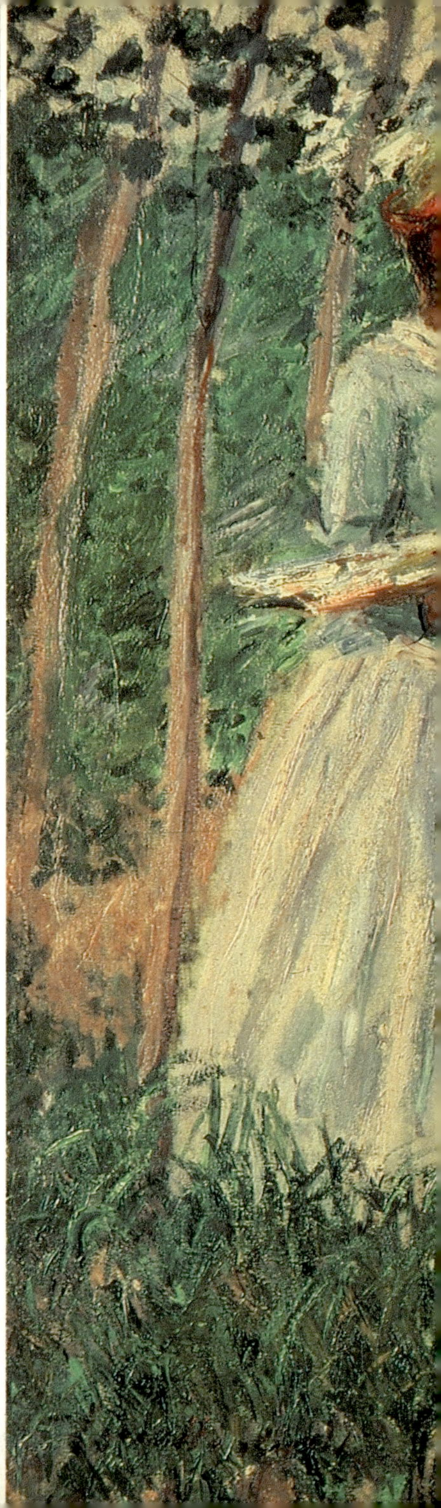

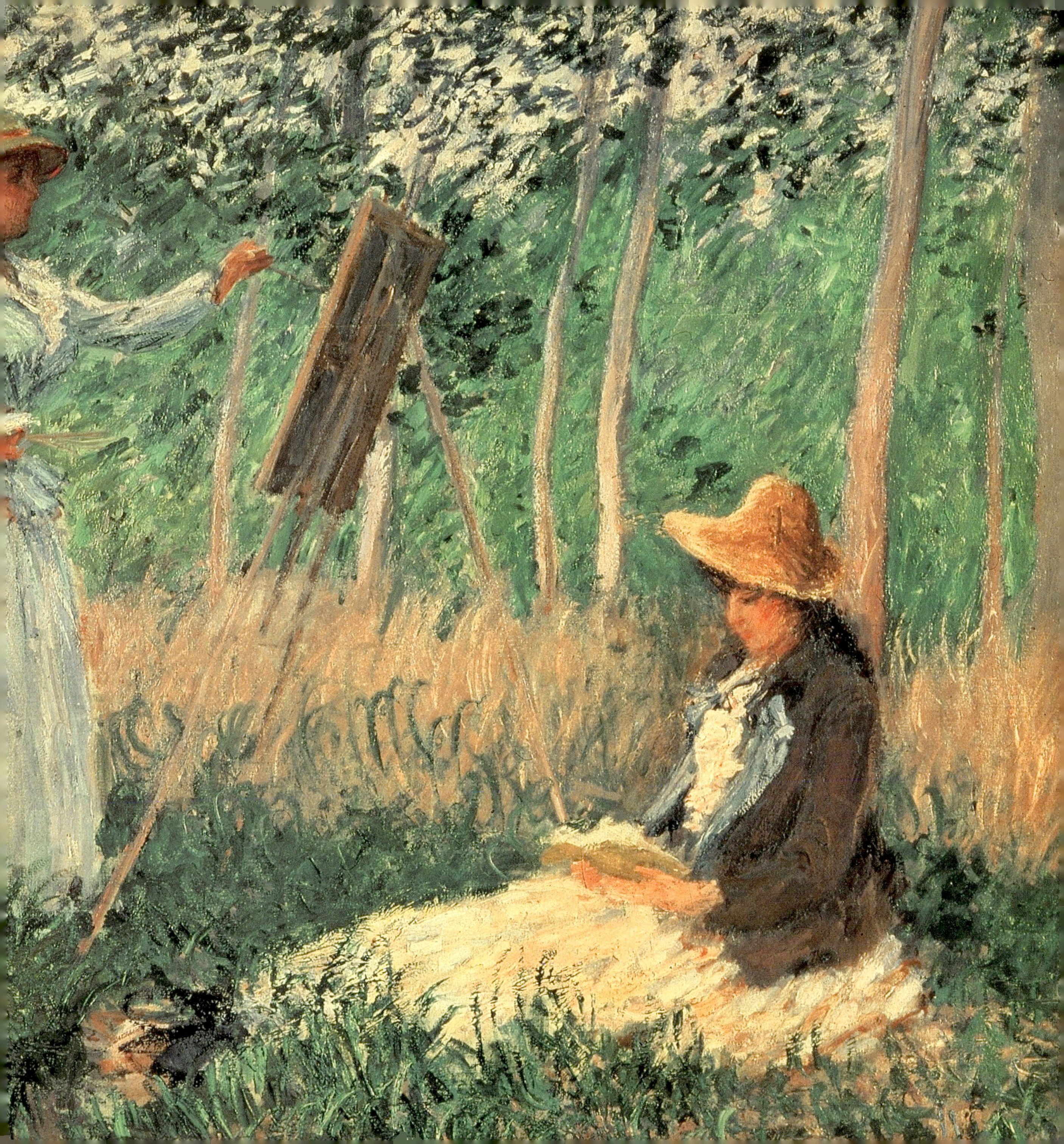

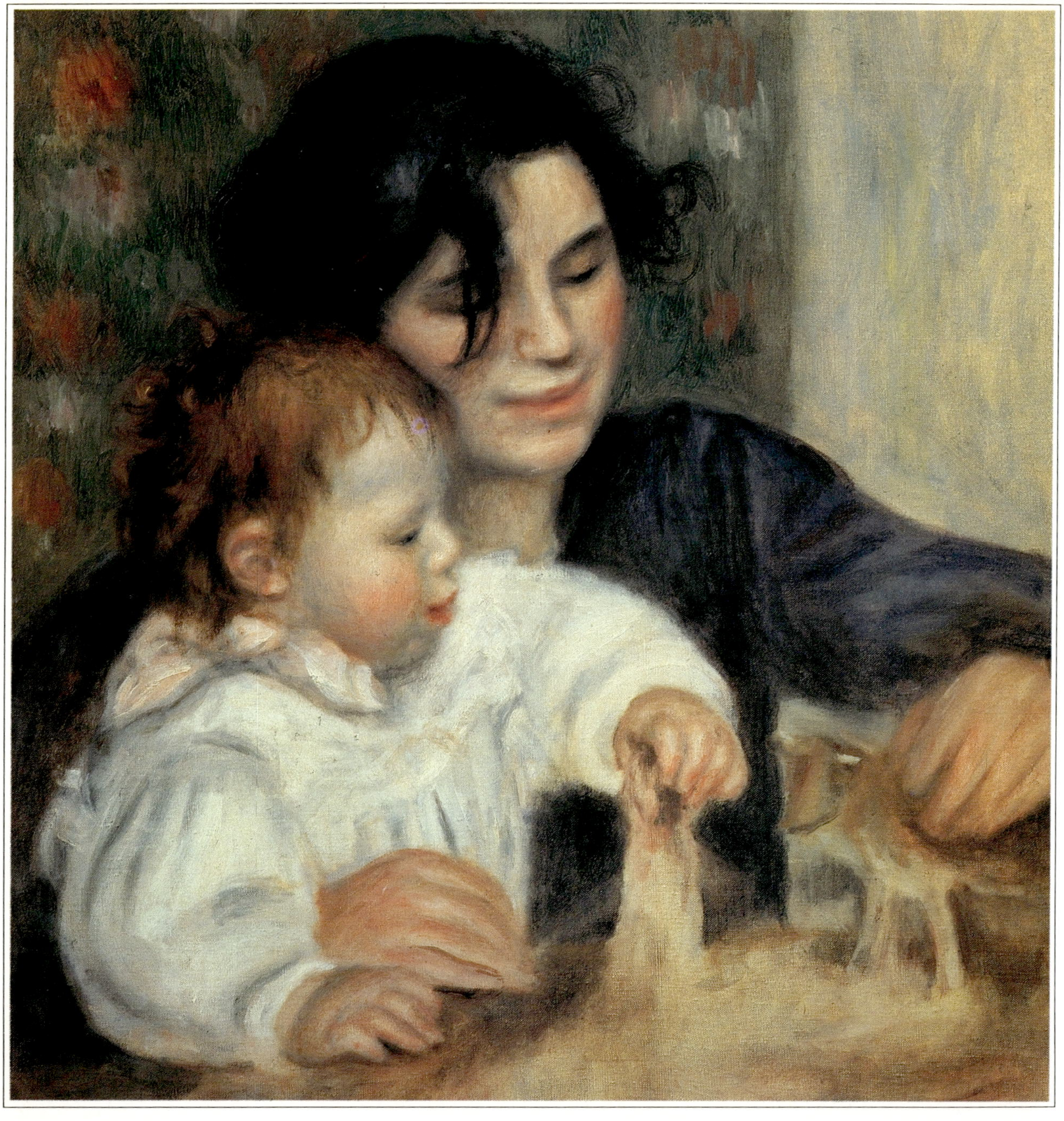

◁ **Gabrielle and Jean**
Pierre-Auguste Renoir
(1841-1919)

Oil on canvas

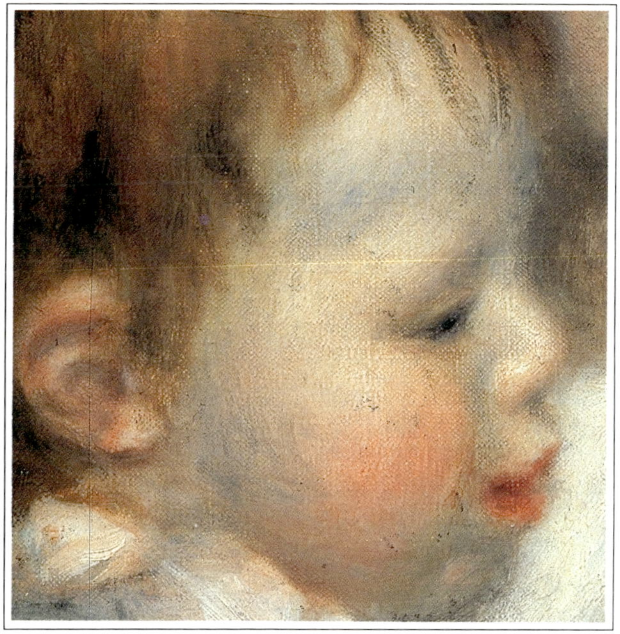

Detail

RENOIR WAS BORN in Limoges, the manufacturing centre of the world-famous French porcelain, and he began his phenomenal artistic career as an apprentice to a porcelain painter. After his marriage to Alice Charigat in 1881, he had three sons: Pierre, Jean and Claude, born in 1885, 1893 and 1901 respectively. The little boy in this charming portrait is the middle son, Jean, who grew up to be a famous film director, many of which became classics of the French cinema. Renoir painted many wonderful portraits of his own and other people's children – the fact that this was his own son does of course lend the portrait reproduced here an extra dimension. Gabrielle, who was a relative and valued friend, company and servant of the family, was often used as a model by Renoir: her striking colouring and wholesome, earthy appearance clearly appealed to him. The portrait of the child in his smock absorbed in playing with a toy farm animal, the loving glance of his companion and the delightful contrast in the size of their hands captures a treasured moment of childhood.

▷ **Mademoiselle Gachet in Her Garden**
Vincent van Gogh (1853-90)

Oil on canvas

VAN GOGH, born in Holland to Dutch parents, considered following his father into the priesthood but instead devoted himself to an artistic career with passionate intensity. His was a tragically turbulent life – after his move from Paris to Arles in the South of France in 1888 he suffered disturbing hallucinations and was interned in hospital at Arles, then in the asylum at St-Rémy. In May 1890 he placed himself under the care of Dr Paul-Ferdinand Gachet in Auvers-sur-Oise. Dr Gachet, who specialized in nervous diseases, was keenly interested in art and was a close friend of a number of painters – Manet was another of his patients. Van Gogh painted portraits of the doctor in his charming home in the rue des Vessenots (now rue Gachet) at Auvers, and on this occasion painted his daughter Marguerite in the Gachets' lovely garden overlooking the Oise valley (another portrait of Marguerite shows her playing the piano). This is such a happy painting – the powerful, confident brushstrokes and characteristic wavy lines and whirling forms capture to perfection the foliage and flowers in a riot of colours around the central figure. Yet only two months later van Gogh shot himself.

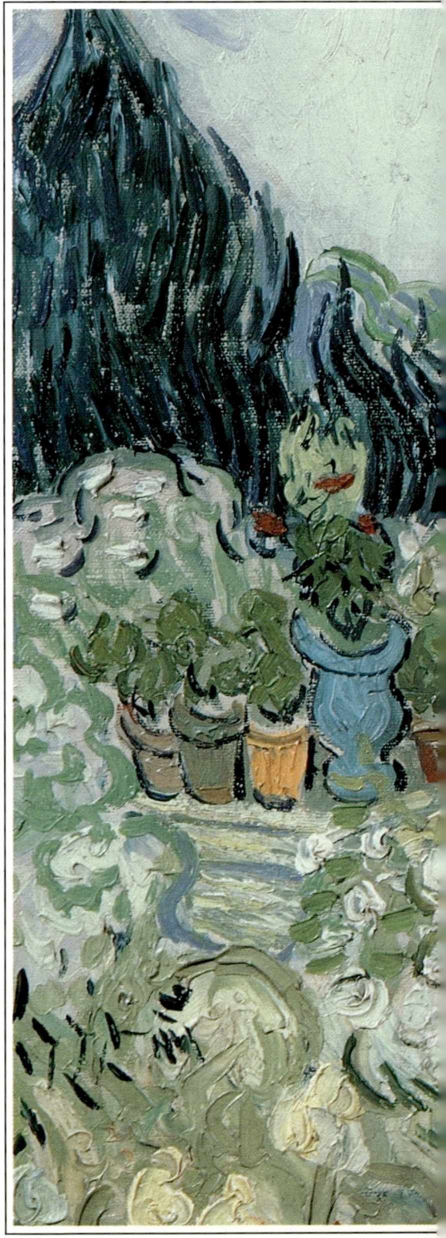

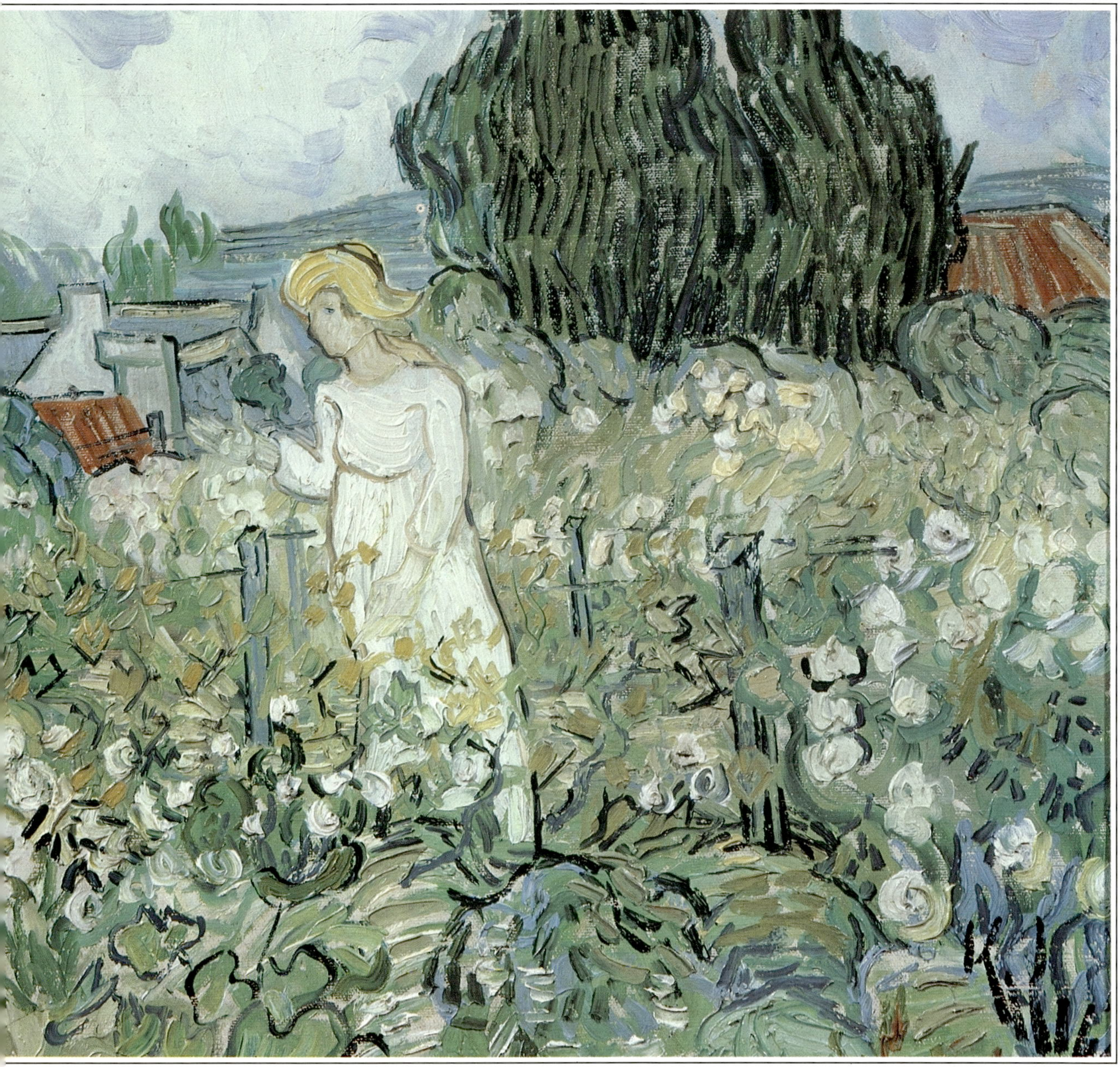

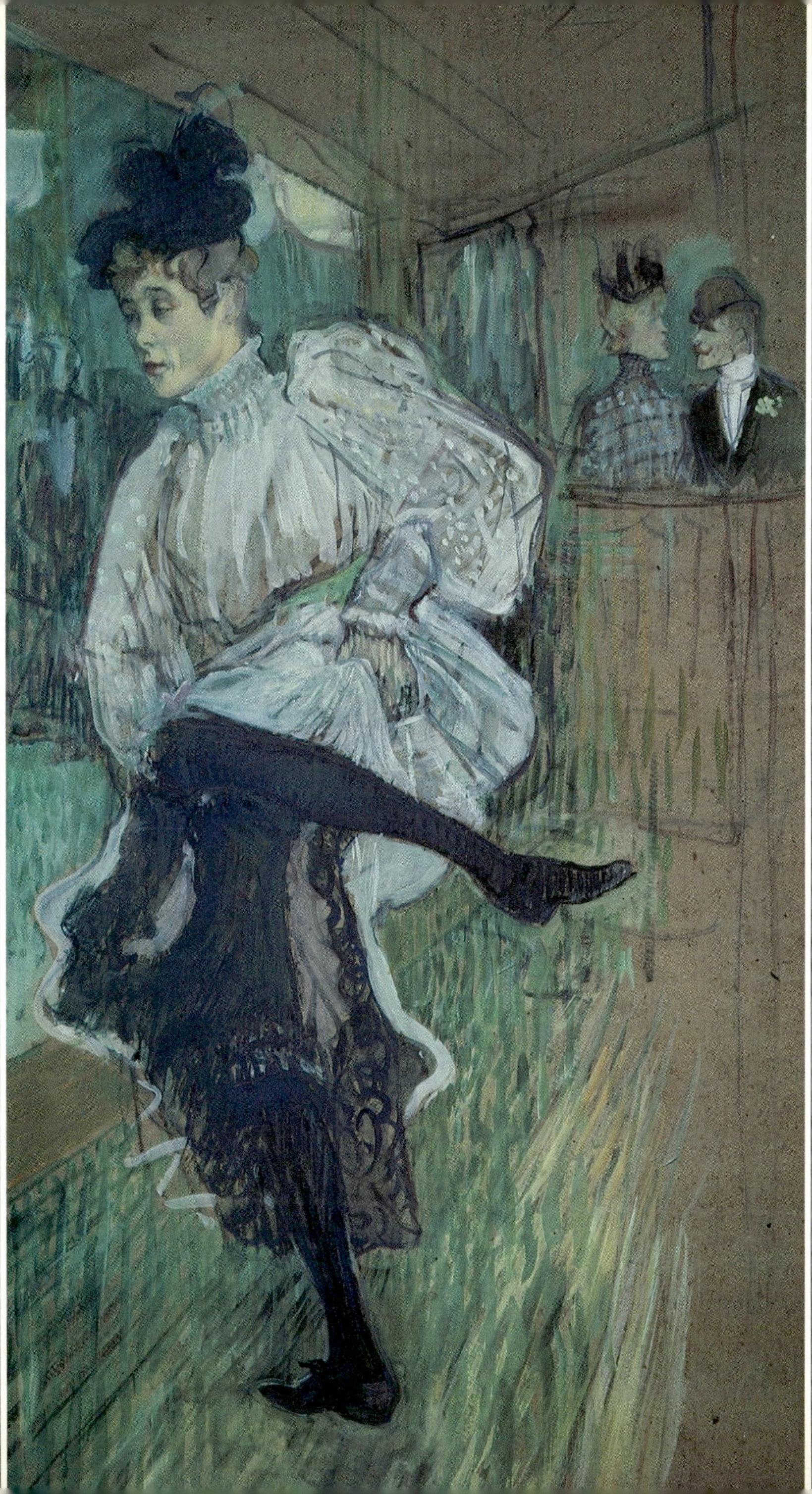

◁ **Jane Avril Dancing**
Henri de Toulouse-Lautrec
(1864-1901)

Oil on canvas

TOULOUSE-LAUTREC was born into an ancient aristocratic family in Albi, where a museum now houses a collection of his works. Two falls in 1878 and 1879 tragically crippled Henri and stunted his growth for life. However, he courageously developed his precocious talent for painting and at 21 was living as an artist in the Montmartre district of Paris. Here he frequented the dance halls and cabarets which epitomized the turn-of-the-century Belle Epoque, using the customers, prostitutes and dancers as his models. The most popular of these venues was the Moulin Rouge. Jane Avril, the daughter of a famous Second Empire courtesan and an Italian nobleman, featured in a number of Lautrec's paintings and posters. She was his friend and confidante and a favourite with the clientele for her blend of depravity and demureness. The man chatting to the girl in the background is William Tom Warrener, Lautrec's subject in *The Englishman at the Moulin Rouge.*

▷ **The New Home**
Walter Sickert (1860-1942)

Oil on canvas

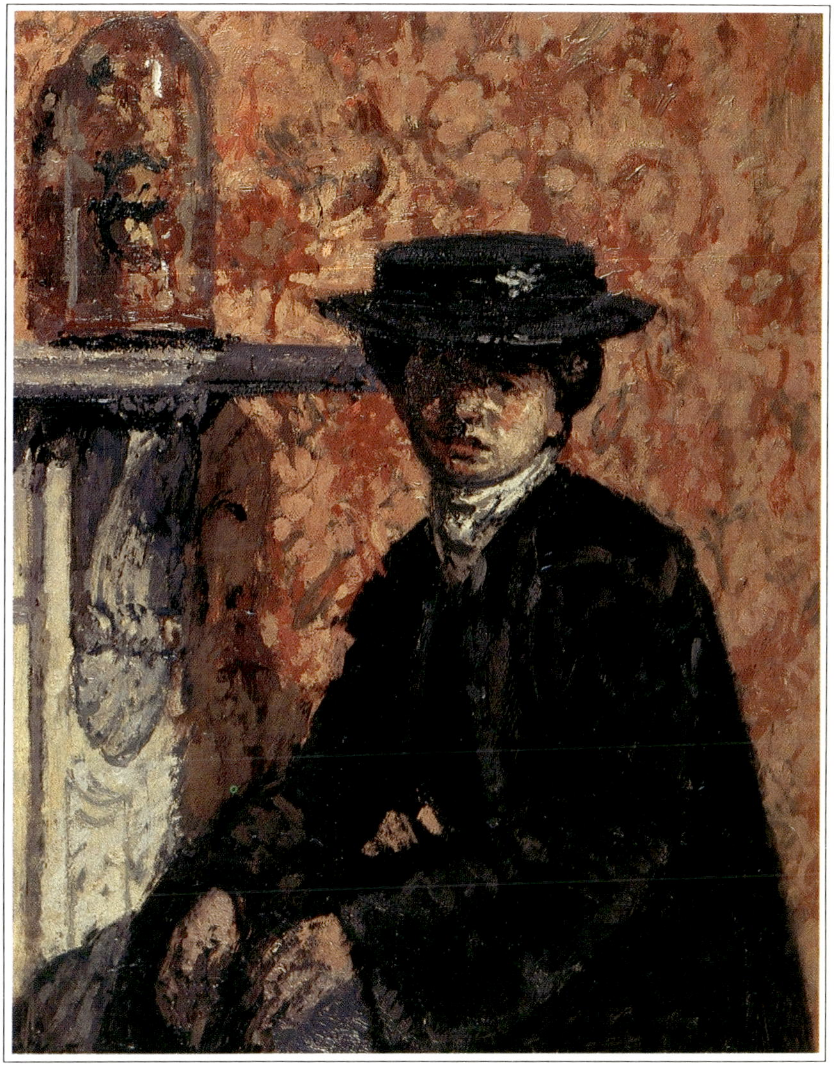

BORN IN MUNICH, Germany, Sickert was apprenticed to Whistler after attending the Slade School of Art in London – it was he who delivered Whistler's portrait of his mother for exhibition at the Salon de Paris in 1883. Sickert was especially famous for his theatre scenes and interiors of low, often sordid life in London's Camden Town, where he lived from 1908 to 1914, renting rooms on the corner of Mornington Crescent and a studio in Fitzroy Street. The district gave its name to the Camden Town Group of artists, of whom Sickert was the leader, later renamed the London Group. Sickert liked to give his portraits theme titles (other examples are *Ennui,* and *What Shall We Do for the Rent?*), and *The New Home* is one such. This half-length portrait of a coster girl wearing a shiny black straw hat was well summed up by a contemporary review in the *Pall Mall Magazine*: 'Here is a young woman ill at ease, apparently her hat not yet removed – her head and bust seen large against the mantelshelf – and she is taking very unkindly to the second-rate, sordid lodging to which she is condemned by an unkindly fate.'

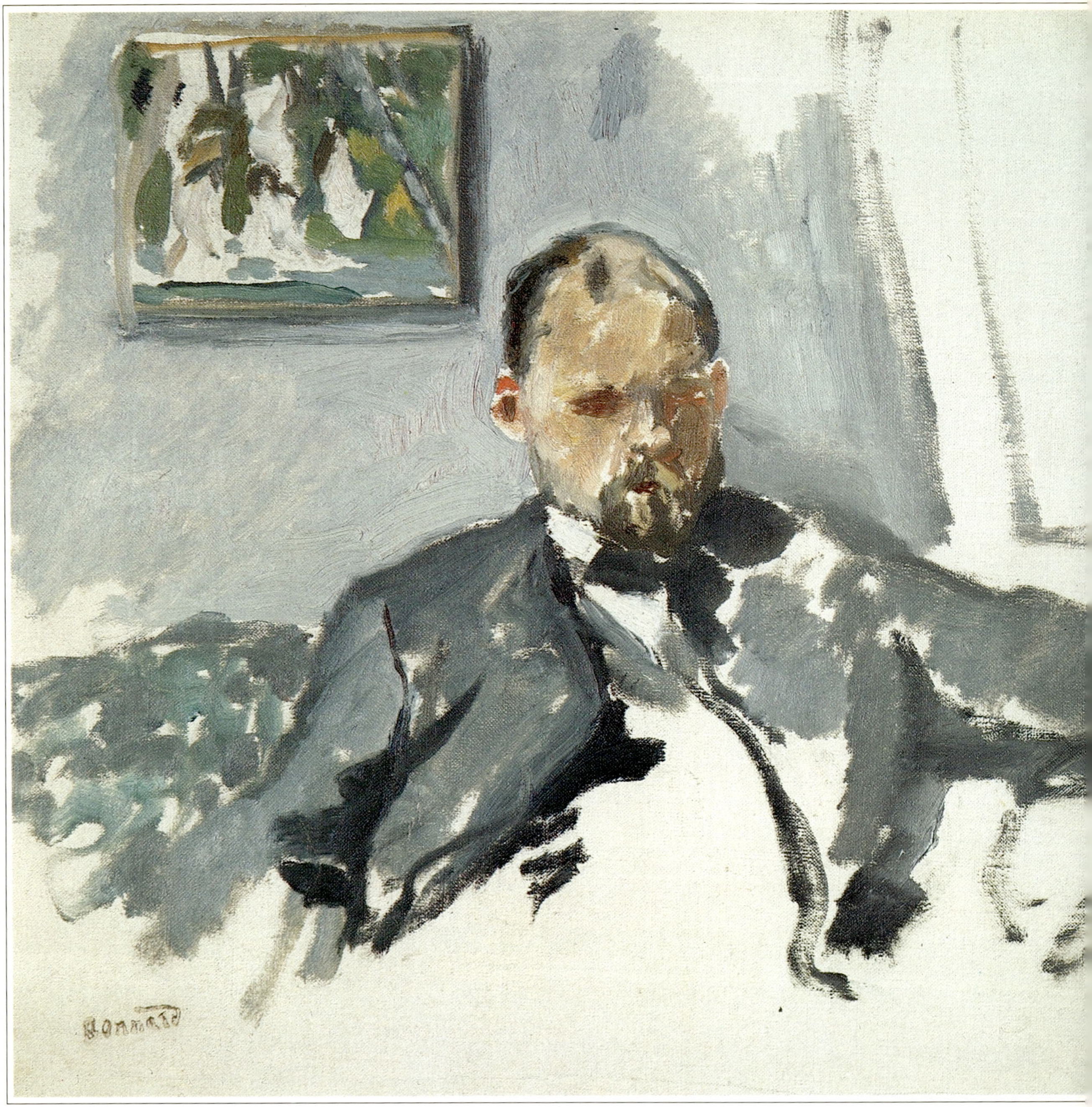

◁ **Ambroise Vollard** Pierre Bonnard (1867-1947)

Oil on canvas

BONNARD WAS A BOOK illustrator, lithographer and stage designer as well as painter, but is best known for his quiet domestic interiors, often showing a woman – always Madame Bonnard, the artist's sole model – reading, dressing, bathing, sleeping, and so on. This portrait of the Paris art dealer Ambroise Vollard is particularly interesting because it is unfinished, and so gives a very good idea of how an artist went about constructing a portrait, concentrating first on the details of the head and face. The picture on the wall is especially significant here, as Vollard was a picture dealer – he had a gallery in the rue Laffitte in Paris. He was highly influential, playing an important part in the careers of a number of leading artists at the turn of the century. Picasso was one of these, from whom Vollard bought paintings, drawings and engravings. In 1910 Picasso painted a portrait of Vollard in the Cubist style, which forms an interesting contrast with Bonnard's.

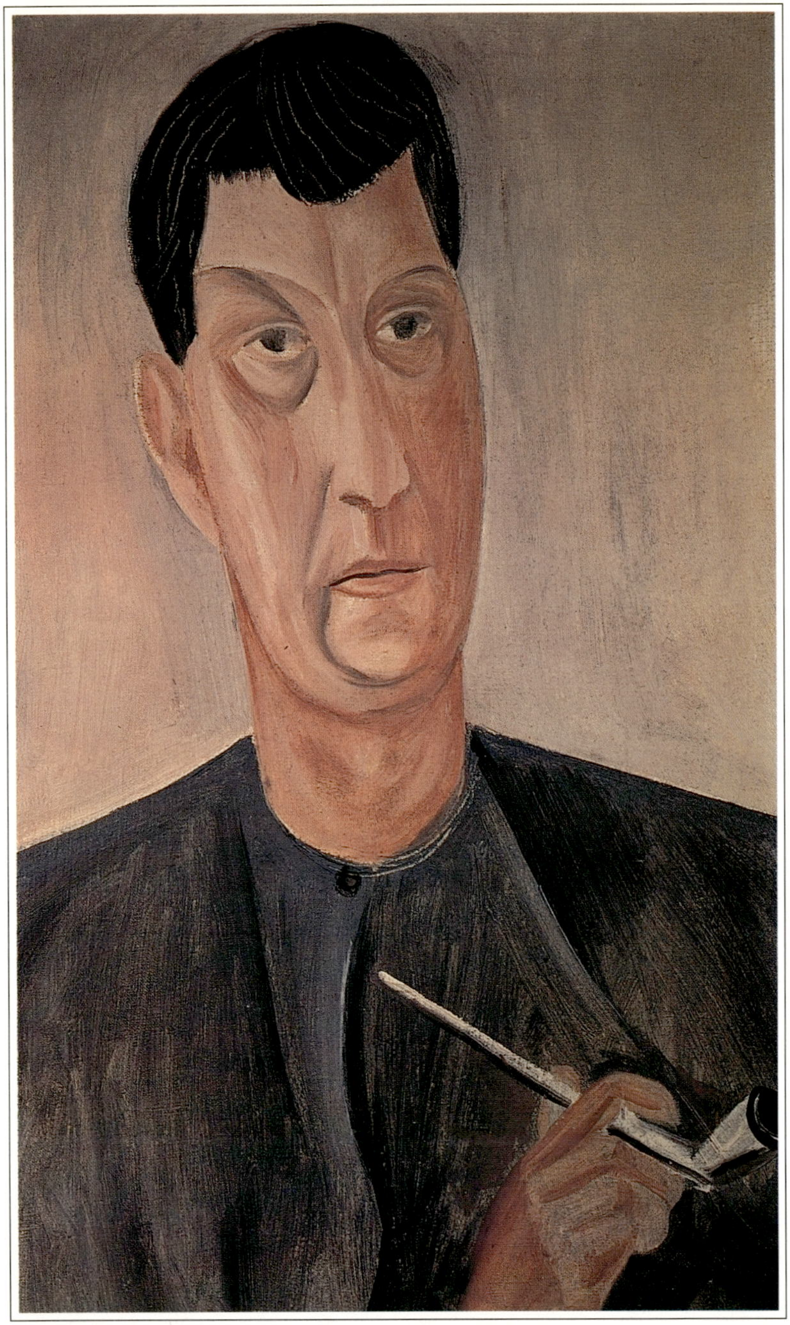

◁ **Self-portrait**
André Derain (1880-1954)

Oil on canvas

DERAIN, TOGETHER WITH Matisse, was foremost among the group of artists known as the Fauves (literally 'wild beasts' in French) who in the first decade of the 20th century caused a sensation with their distorted, violently coloured paintings. Matisse painted a portrait of Derain in a sailor's cap, portrayed in typically vivid colours, but there are none of these in this self-portrait; instead, Derain has used the restrained colours he turned to just before 1920, favouring browns and olive-green. In this way he has given his portrait a serious, sober, thoughtful feel, reinforced by the reflective pose with the long-stemmed pipe. This is a very good example of the kind of self-portrait in which the artist appears to be taking a long, critical look at himself. It is an exercise in appraisal, an attempt both to discover something new about his own personality and to explore some of the endless possibilities of expression offered to an artist by the human face.

▷ **Mother and Child**
Pablo Picasso (1881-1973)

Oil on canvas

Born in Malaga, Spain, Picasso had already gone through his Blue and Rose periods by the time he painted this portrait in the summer of 1907. Picasso adored children and painted and drew innumerable portraits of his own. He had already explored the mother-child relationship in an oil of 1901, *Mother and Child (Maternity),* in a pastel of 1903, a drawing of 1904 and a gouache of 1905. Whole sequences of images of maternity would follow in the early 1920s to celebrate the birth of Picasso's son Paul and in 1935 after his daughter Maia was born. The portrait reproduced here portrays all the closeness of the bonding process, as the mother nuzzles her baby's head. The style reflects Picasso's special interest at the time in primitive ancient Iberian art and African Negro sculpture and wooden masks. The mother's long oval face, large eyes, elongated nose and navel-shaped mouth are all highly reminiscent of these masks.

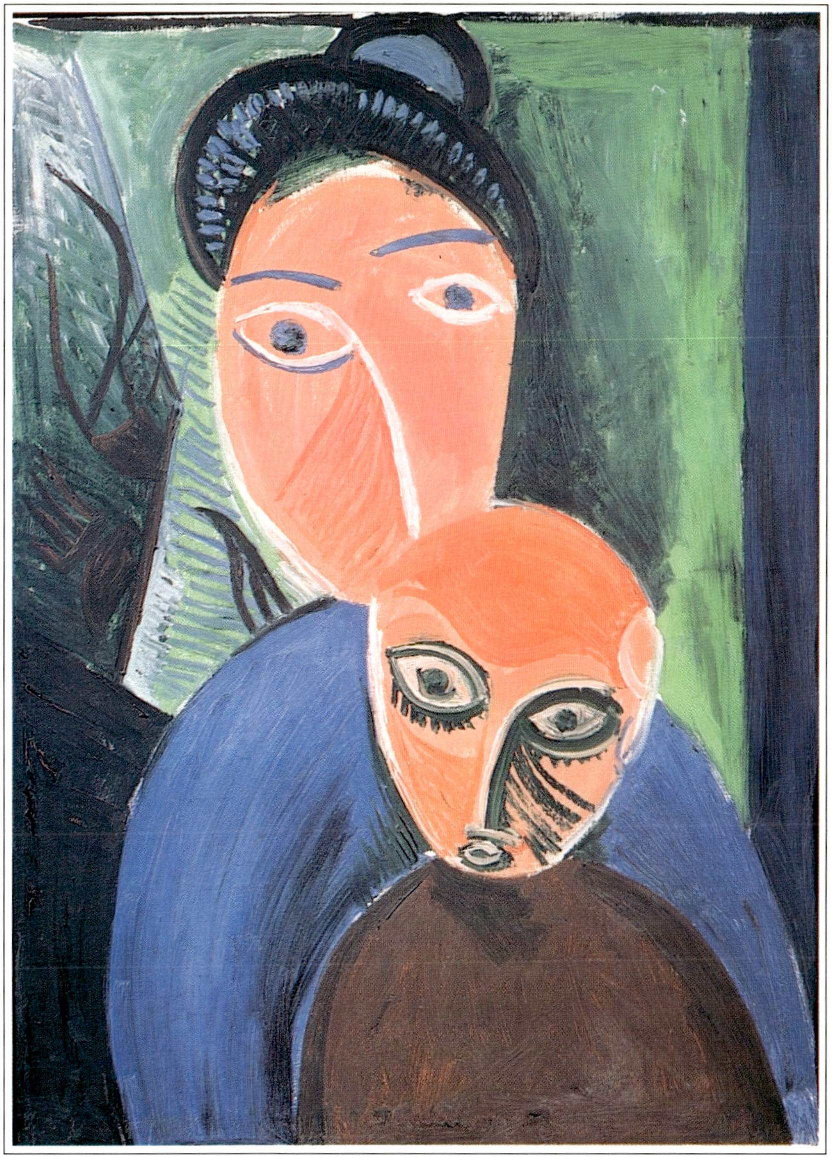

▷ **Jeanne Hébuterne in a Yellow Jumper**
Amedeo Modigliani
(1884-1920)

Oil on canvas

THE CAREER OF MODIGLIANI was cut tragically short by his death from tuberculosis, aggravated by drug and alcohol abuse. Modigliani, who came from a distinguished Italian-Jewish family, was a great humanitarian, a champion of the impoverished and socially disadvantaged, and his work is moving in its reflection of his natural compassion. He painted numerous portraits of ordinary men and women and also of celebrities, such as the artist Chaim Soutine and the writer Jean Cocteau. Modigliani often used his mistress Jeanne Hébuterne as a model; she committed suicide on the evening of the day of his death, unable to contemplate life without him. Modigliani was above all a superb draughtsman and used line to wonderful effect in his portraits to explore the personalities of his sitters and express his own feeling for them.

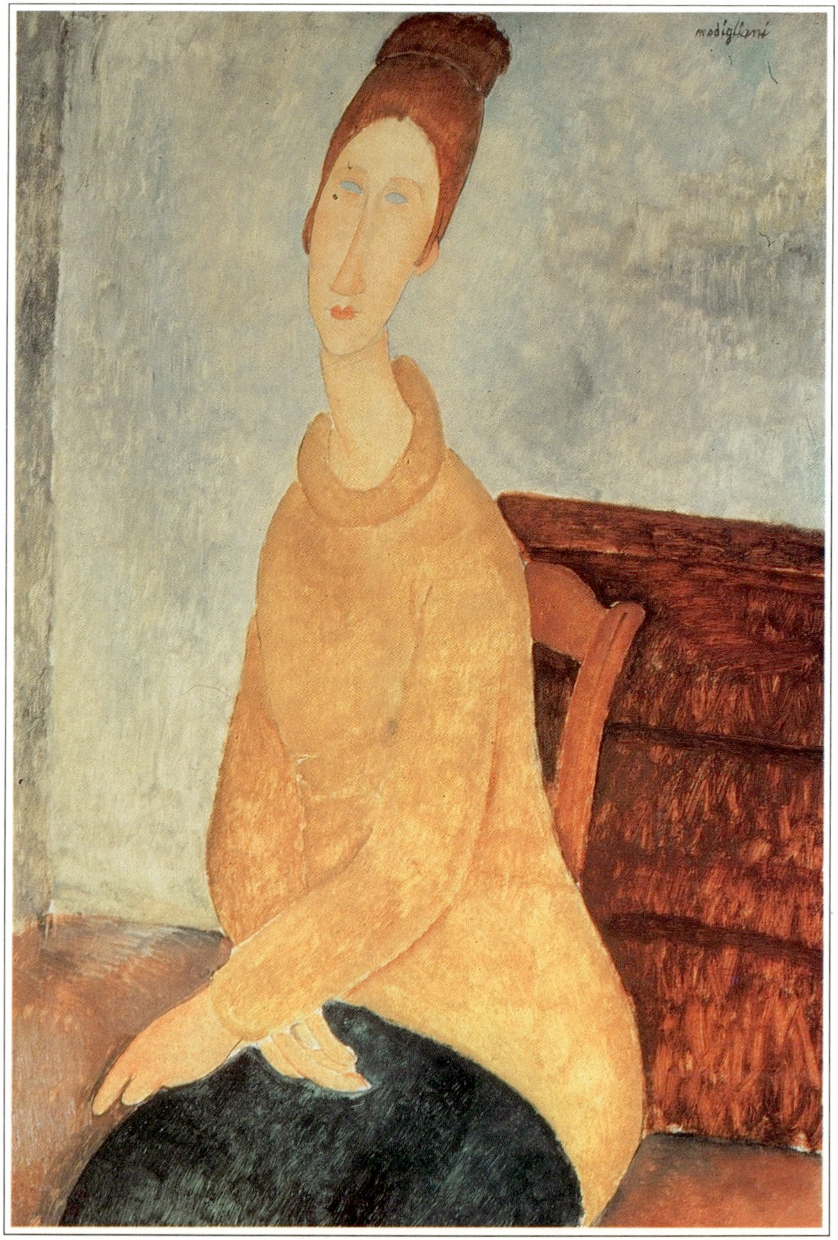

▷ **Woman with Head Full of Cloud** Salvador Dali (1904-89)

Oil

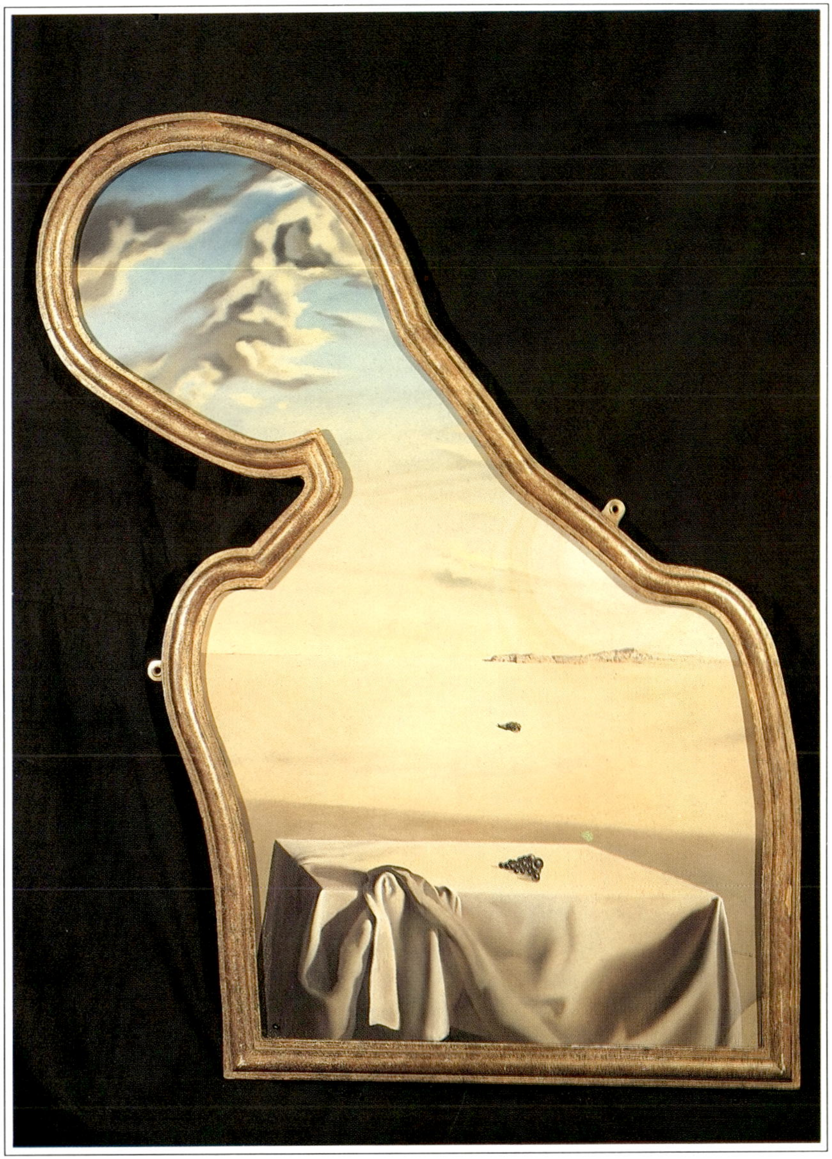

DALI'S FLAMBOYANT, unpredictable personality, his technical brilliance and extraordinary imagination made him one of the artists most popularly associated with the Surrealist movement. It is often hard to tell where madness begins and genius ends in his work. In 1929 he met Gala, wife of the poet Paul Eluard: she became a constant inspiration and Dali painted her again and again: the couple married in 1958. Dali believed that he had become two people by his union with Gala, a belief which he expressed lyrically in a pair of portraits with a cosmic feel, *Couple with Heads Full of Cloud,* in 1934. The portrait of the woman, reproduced here, leans romantically towards the man's, the frame following the contour of her shoulders, neck and head. In the background is the tiny rocky bay of Port Lligat in Cadaqués, where Gala and Dali lived in a house by the water.

▷ **Marilyn** Andy Warhol (1930-87)

Silkscreen

WARHOL, BORN IN 1928, was a central figure in pop art, the term coined to describe works of art whose sources lay in the products of the mass media. From 1960 (before which he worked as an illustrator and commercial artist), Warhol began to make paintings based on comic-strip characters like Popeye and Batman, mass-produced objects like Coca Cola bottles and Campbells soup tins, and photographs of celebrities. He would hand-paint his images, then reproduce them multiply or singly by means of the silkscreen process. He chose to give this treatment to Marilyn Monroe, who had become an icon of the 20th century by means of mass media communication: movies like *Gentlemen Prefer Blondes, Niagara, Bus Stop* and *Some Like It Hot* had fixed her as a universal star in the public consciousness. Marilyn died in 1962, the year of Warhol's depiction of her. At her funeral her drama coach Lee Strasberg said of her: 'She had a luminous quality – a combination of wistfulness, radiance and yearning that set her apart and yet made everyone wish to be part of it.' It is exactly these qualities that Warhol has captured here.

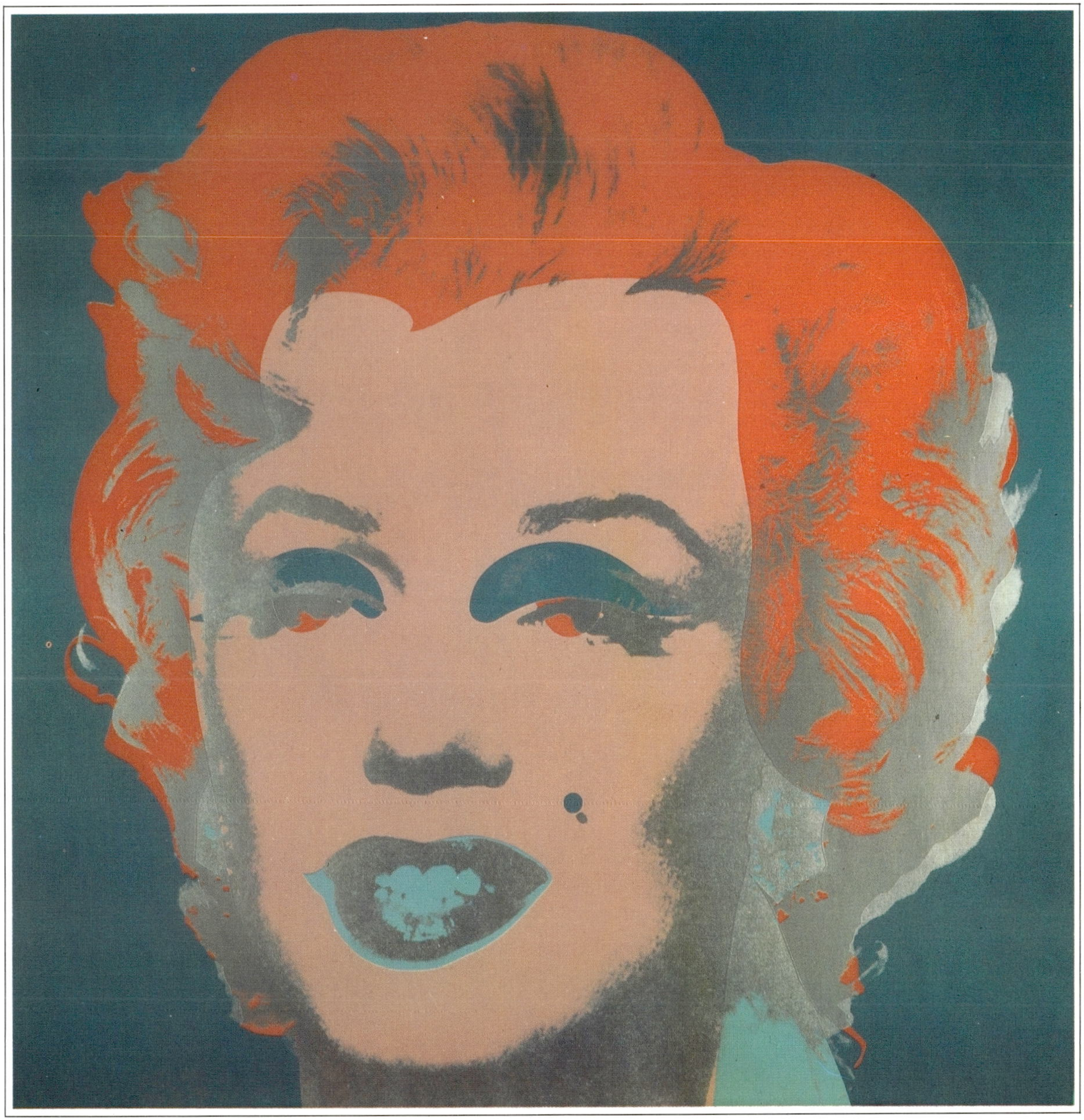

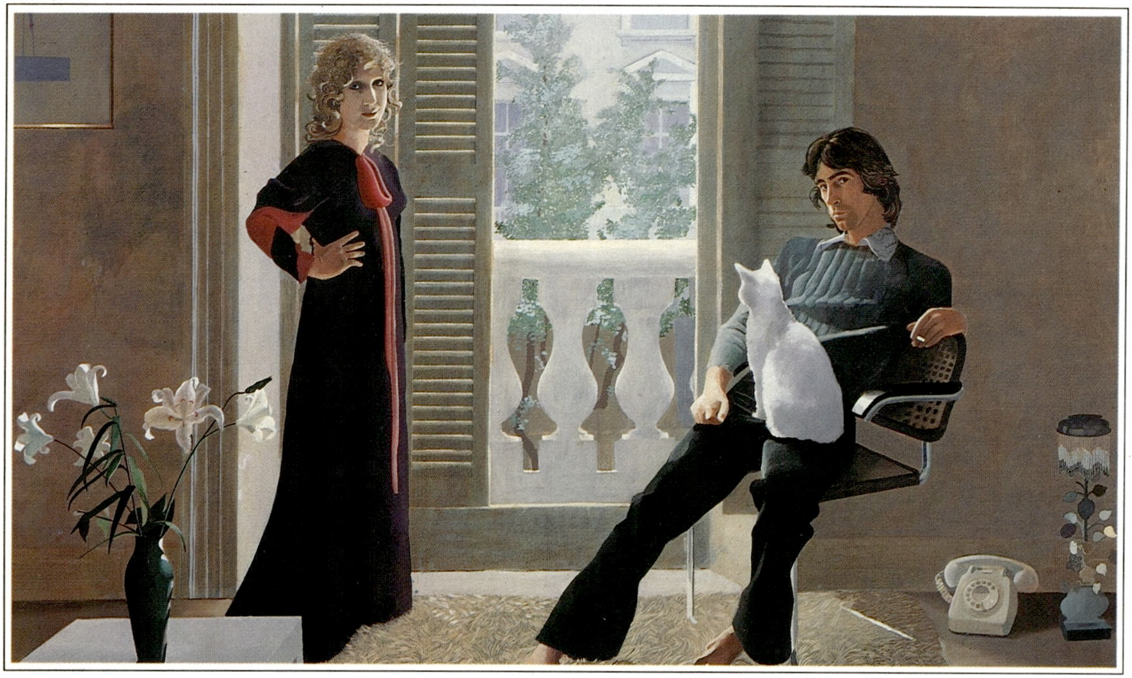

△ **Mr and Mrs Clark with Percy** David Hockney (1937-)

Acrylic on canvas

AFTER ATTENDING ART SCHOOL in his native Bradford, in Yorkshire, Hockey studied at the Royal College of Art in London before moving to Los Angeles in 1964. In the late 60s he painted a number of portraits of couples which reflect his special interest in their relationship: one of his parents, others of his friends Christopher Isherwood and Don Bachardy, and of the American collectors Fred and Marcia Weisman. This double portrait of the fashion designer Ossie Clark and his wife, the fabric designer Celia Birtwell, falls into the same category. Hockney uses the acrylic paints with which he experimented on first moving to California to create marvellous effects of colour, light and shade. Sunlight floods through the louvred balcony doors but inside the room is cool and casually elegant, the perfect setting for such a stylish and successful couple. Their pose conveys the impression that this husband and wife are independent, forceful people, successful in their own right. The cat remains totally aloof, with his back to the artist, looking intently out at the garden beyond the stucco balcony.

ACKNOWLEDGEMENTS

The Publisher would like to thank the following for their kind permission to reproduce the paintings in this book:

Bridgeman Art Library, London/Alte Pinakotheck, Munich 10; /**Burghley House, Stamford, Lincolnshire** 19; /**Château de Versailles, France** 33; /**Chatsworth House, Derbyshire** 42; /**Christie's, London** 24; /**Christopher Wood Gallery, London** 60; /**Crown Estate, Institute of Directors** 27; /**Ex-Edward James Foundation, Sussex** 75; /**The Fine Art Society, London** 69; /**Fondazione Contini-Bonacossi, Florence** 14; /**Giraudon/Kurpfalzisches Museum, Heidelberg** 11; /**Giraduon/Louvre, Paris** 9, 13, 20, 54; /**Giraudon/Pollock House Museum, Glasgow** 16; /**Giraudon/Musée d'Orsay, Paris** 58-59, 64, 66-67, 68; /**Giraudon/Prado, Madrid** 50; /**Hermitage, St Petersburg** 26; /**Historical Society of Pennsylvania, USA** 45; /**Los Angeles County Museum of Art** 62-63; /**Louvre, Paris** 32; /**Manor House, Stanton Harcourt, Oxon** 29; /**Mauritshuis, The Hague** 25; /**Musée Picasso, Paris** 73; /**National Gallery, London** 8, 30-31, 40; /**National Gallery of Art, Washington DC** 28; /**National Museum of American Art, Smithsonian Inst.** 51; /**Neue Pinakothek, Munich** 56; /**Palais de Tokyo, Paris** 70-71; /**Philip Mould Historical Portraits Ltd, London**43; /**Phillips, The International Fine Art Auctioneers** 77; /**Prado, Madrid** 22-23, 47; /**Private Collection**34-35, 72;/**Royal Holloway and Bedford New College** 55; /**Schloss Charlottenburg, Berlin** 48; /**Solomon R. Guggenheim Museum, New York** 74; /**Tate Gallery, London** 61, 78; /**Victoria and Albert Museum** 17; /**Wallace Collection, London** 36; /**Wolverhampton Art Gallery, Staffs** 38-39.